Table of Contents P9-DVB-855

Devotions
for
Little Boys and Girls

Jesus and His Friends

by Joan C. Webb
illustrations by R. Max Kolding

STANDARD
PUBLISHING
Cincinnati, Ohio

Dedicated to my children, Lynnette and Rich

The Standard Publishing Company, Cincinnati, Ohio
A division of Standex International Corporation
Text © 1995 by Joan C. Webb
Illustrations © 1995 by The Standard Publishing Company
All rights reserved.
Printed in the United States of America
02 01 00 99 98 97 96 95   5 4 3 2 1

Library of Congress Catalog Card Number 94-067874
ISBN 0-7847-0295-0
Cataloging-in-Publication Data available
Designed by Coleen Davis

Scripture from the International Children's Bible, New Century Version,
© 1986, 1989 by Word Publishing, Dallas, Texas 75039.
Used by permission.

Dear parents, grandparents, and teachers,

Jesus is the young child's friend. While he was here on earth, he expressed love and concern for the welfare of children. He valued the simple faith of a child and encouraged adults to nurture and protect that faith. We parents, grandparents, and teachers have a unique privilege. When we share the message of Jesus, we introduce our children to God and his plan for life. I've written this book of simple Bible-based devotions entitled *Jesus and His Friends* to help you teach about Jesus' life and relationships. The one-page devotions include stories about Jesus' Bible-times friends as well as stories about contemporary children who are friends of Jesus.

Each one-page devotion begins with a verse to think about and concludes with follow-up in the form of questions, suggested activities, and a prayer. Many of the simple activities encourage quiet learning times. For active interaction you may wish to do the more involved suggested activities.

This book is intended for young children three to seven years old. You or your child may write his name on the blank provided within each devotion. In this way, the book becomes uniquely individual. To encourage further participation, you may have your child draw a happy face or place a sticker at the top of the page to celebrate completing each story and/or activity.

I hope you and your child have fun reading these stories together and that they help initiate a lifelong friendship with Jesus.

— *Joan C. Webb*

BELIEVING GOD
Luke 1:8-22

Don't be afraid; only believe. Mark 5:36

_____ , have you ever had to wait for Mom or Dad to pick you up at school or church? Did you wonder what happened? Long ago the people waited for one of their leaders, Zechariah, to come out of the temple-church. "What's taking so long?" they asked. "Is he all right?"

When Zechariah finally came out of the temple, he couldn't talk. He made signs with his hands. The people guessed that something special had happened while Zechariah was in the temple.

That special something was a visit from an angel! "You and your wife, Elizabeth, are going to have a baby," said the angel. "He will grow up to be a great man for the Lord. God wants him to tell people to get ready for Jesus to come."

"That can't be. My wife and I are too old to have a baby," said Zechariah.

"Oh, yes, it's true, Zechariah," said the angel. "You wonder if you can really believe this, don't you? Well, you're going to lose your voice until the day your son is born. What I've told you is true. Believe me. This message is from God."

Questions
1. Who waited for Zechariah to come out? (The people)
2. Who talked to Zechariah? (An angel)
3. Did Zechariah believe the angel at first? (No)

Activities
1. Sign the word "baby" by rocking your arms back and forth.
2. Try to make each other understand what you want to say without talking aloud.

Prayer
Dear God, I want to believe what you tell me in the Bible. Please help me not to be afraid. Amen.

MARY AND THE ANGEL
Luke 1:26-38

Mary said, ". . . Let this happen to me as you say!"
Luke 1:38

"Hi, Mary. God is happy with you. He is with you."

Mary looked up to see God's special angel. "What does all this mean?" she wondered.

"Don't be afraid," said Gabriel. "God has chosen you to be the mother of his son."

"Tell me how this will happen," said Mary. "I'm not even married yet."

"God has a plan, Mary," said the angel. "His spirit will come on you. You will be pregnant. The baby will be God's own perfect Son. I know this is hard to understand, but remember, God can do anything."

"I'm God's servant," Mary said. "I want to do what he wants me to do."

_____ , Mary decided to do what God asked her to do. She made a good choice. We, too, can decide to become God's men and women, boys and girls.

Questions
1. What was the angel's name? (Gabriel)
2. Whom did God choose to be the mother of his Son? (Mary)
3. Did Mary decide to do what God wanted her to do? (Yes)

Activities
1. Color the picture on the next page.
2. Find pictures of mothers-to-be in a magazine.

Prayer
Dear God, I want to do whatever you ask me to do, just like Mary. Help me to know what you want me to do now and when I grow up. Amen.

VISITING ELIZABETH
Luke 1:39-56

Let us praise his name together. *Psalm 34:3*

_____ , do you like to visit Aunt _____ ? It's fun going to her house, isn't it? Mary liked visiting Elizabeth.

The angel Gabriel told Mary that Elizabeth was going to have a baby, too. "Elizabeth and I can talk together about our babies," Mary said. She went to see Elizabeth.

"Mary, how wonderful to see you!" Elizabeth said as she opened the door. "God told me about your baby boy. He's the Son of God. God is happy that you believed the angel's words."

Mary said, "How I thank and praise God for choosing me to have his Son. God is very good to me."

Mary stayed with Elizabeth for three months. Maybe they made blankets or sewed tiny clothes for their babies. Then Mary kissed Elizabeth good-bye and went back to her own home. Both Mary and Elizabeth loved God. They praised God and sang together.

Questions
1. Whom did Mary visit? (Elizabeth)
2. Who told Elizabeth that Mary was going to have a baby? (God)
3. How long did Mary stay with Elizabeth? (Three months)

Activities
1. Look at three months on a calendar. Count to ninety (three months of days).
2. Draw a picture of the little clothes that Elizabeth and Mary might have made for their babies.

Prayer
Dear God, Mary thanked you for choosing her to have baby Jesus. Her heart was happy. My heart is happy, too, because you chose me to be your child. Thank you. Amen.

GROWING UP
Luke 1:64-80

We will grow up in every way to be like Christ. *Ephesians 4:15*

After baby John was born, Zechariah began to talk again just like the angel promised. The first words that Zechariah said were words of prayer and praise to God. "Wow! Listen to Zechariah," said the people. "He has his voice back!"

"Thank you, God. You're so good to us," prayed Zechariah. He knew God had a special plan for his son John. Zechariah leaned down to kiss his baby boy. "You, my child, will grow up to be God's special helper," he whispered.

Every day little John grew taller and stronger — just like you, _____ . When John became a man, he lived in the desert and waited for the right time to start telling people to get ready for Jesus. John grew up to love God. He decided to obey what God told him to do. You can grow up to love and obey God, too.

Questions
1. What did Zechariah do when he got his voice back? (He prayed.)
2. Who grew up strong? (John)
3. Where did John live while he waited to tell people about Jesus? (In the desert)

Activities
1. Measure your child to see how tall he is.
2. Make and display a chart to keep track of your child's monthly physical growth.

Prayer
Dear God, John grew up to be strong and tall. He also grew to love you. I'm growing up, too. Help me to grow strong and tall. I want to grow to love you, too. Amen.

THE "ADOPTED" DAD
Matthew 1:18-25

You are the Christ, the Son of the living God. *Matthew 16:16*

_____ , have you ever been to a wedding? Mary and Joseph were planning a wedding. They loved each other and wanted to be married. Joseph was a good man. Mary looked forward to being his wife.

One night before the wedding, an angel from God talked to Joseph in a dream. In the dream an angel said, "Joseph, your Mary is going to have a baby. Don't be afraid, though. Everything will be all right. This is God's plan. God is the baby's father. The baby's name will be Jesus. No one will ever be like him."

Joseph believed all that the angel told him. So Joseph and Mary were married. When baby Jesus was born, Joseph became Jesus' "adopted" dad. That means God chose Joseph to love and care for Jesus while he lived here on earth.

Joseph was happy to have Jesus in his family. Joseph loved Jesus. He helped Mary take care of baby Jesus.

Questions
1. Who planned to be married? (Mary and Joseph)
2. What happened to Joseph before the wedding? (An angel from God talked to him in a dream.)
3. Who was Jesus' "adopted" dad? (Joseph)

Activities
1. Show your wedding pictures to your child.
2. Play make-believe wedding with your child, pretending to be Mary and Joseph.

Prayer
Dear God, I know you are Jesus' father. He is your Son. Thank you, though, for giving Jesus his "adopted" father, Joseph, to take care of him when he was a boy. Amen.

HAPPY BIRTHDAY, JESUS
Luke 2:1-20

Today your Savior was born. *Luke 2:11*

_____ , whose birthday do we celebrate at Christmastime? Yes, Jesus' birthday. Jesus' birthday is a special day. No one else in the whole world has so many parties on his birthday. Boys and girls, moms and dads, grandmas and grandpas from many countries remember Jesus on his birthday. But on the day Jesus was born, only a few people celebrated.

Mary and Joseph were tired after a long trip. They couldn't find a place to stay for the night. "Joseph, let's hurry," said Mary. "I think it's almost time for baby Jesus to be born."

Mary and Joseph finally stopped to rest in a stable, where animals were kept. That very night, baby Jesus was born. Mary hugged and fed Jesus. She wrapped him in warm blankets. Then Mary and Joseph made a little bed for Jesus in the animal's feeding box, called a manger.

In a nearby field, an angel visited some shepherds. "Today your Savior was born," said the angel. "Go. Look for the sleeping baby in a manger." And they did. The shepherds were Jesus' first friends and visitors here on earth.

Questions
1. Who has more parties on his birthday than anyone else in the world? (Jesus)
2. Where was Jesus born? (In a stable, where animals were kept)
3. Who were Jesus' first visitors here on earth? (The shepherds)

Activity
Sing "Happy Birthday" to Jesus, even if it isn't Christmastime.

Prayer
Dear God, thank you for sending baby Jesus so many years ago. I know Jesus grew up to be our Savior and our friend. Amen.

GOD LOVES YOUNG AND OLD
Luke 2:36-38

I have trusted you since I was young. *Psalm 71:5*

Anna was eighty-four years old. She loved God. Every day and night in the temple-church, she talked to God in prayer. One day when she looked up after praying, she saw her friend Simeon holding baby Jesus. She hurried over. While Simeon held Jesus in his arms, Anna thanked God. "This child is God's Son, the one we've been praying and waiting for so long," she said. "Thank you, Father God." Anna wanted everyone to know that baby Jesus was God's Son. Anna praised and thanked God.

_____ , how old are you? How old is Grandma (or Grandpa)? Anna was old enough to be your great-grandma. Did you know that a person's age doesn't make any difference to God? Anyone can praise and pray to God. God is happy whenever we pray to him. Young children like you, moms and dads, and grandmas and grandpas can all praise God.

Questions
1. Who prayed in the temple every day and night? (Anna)
2. How old was Anna? (Eighty-four years old)

Activities
1. Look through magazines to find pictures of older people, babies, and small children. Collect these pictures and make a collage. Glue the pictures to a large sheet of paper. Write, "All people, young and old, can praise God."
2. Send a note or picture to an elderly friend or relative.

Prayer
Dear God, little children praise you. And older people like Anna praise you, too. You like to hear our prayers. Help me remember that. Amen.

FOLLOW THAT STAR!
Matthew 2:1-10

Let there be lights in the sky. . . . These lights will be used for signs.
Genesis 1:14

_____ , what do you see in the sky on a clear night? Lots of stars, right? One night long ago, a special star shone brightly in the sky. Wise men who studied about the stars saw this special one. "That must be the star that means a new king is born," they said. "Let's find him and worship him."

When King Herod heard that the wise men were looking for Jesus, he got jealous. "Maybe this new king will grow up and try to take *my* kingdom away," muttered Herod. "People might obey and follow him instead of me. I have to do something about this."

Herod had a plan. He called the wise men to a secret meeting. "The Scripture says this new king will be born in Bethlehem," he told them. "Find him. Then come back and tell me so I can go worship him, too." But King Herod lied. He didn't really want to worship Jesus.

The wise men left the secret meeting and followed the star. It moved in the sky until it stopped over a house in Bethlehem. Inside the house they found Jesus and his mother, Mary. The wise men knew God sent Jesus. They gave Jesus gifts and bowed down to pray.

Questions
1. What did the wise men follow in the sky? (A special star)
2. Where did the star lead them? (To Bethlehem where Jesus lived)

Activity
Sing "Twinkle, Twinkle, Shiny Star" to the tune of "Twinkle, Twinkle, Little Star."

Prayer
Dear God, you made the stars. Thanks for making this special one to be a sign for the wise men to find Jesus. They came to worship and praise Jesus. I worship and praise Jesus, too. Amen.

A TRIP IN THE NIGHT
Matthew 2:12-18

God will take care of you. *Genesis 50:24*

After the wise men visited little Jesus at his house, they had a dream. In the dream, God warned them *not* to go back to King Herod. God knew Herod wanted to kill young Jesus. God wanted to keep Jesus and his family safe. The wise men went home another way.

When the wise men didn't come back, King Herod got angry. "I'm going to find this child. And I'll get rid of him," said King Herod.

But an angel came to Jesus' adopted dad, Joseph. "Herod is looking for Jesus. He wants to hurt him," said the angel. "Get up and take Jesus and Mary to Egypt. Stay there until I tell you what to do." So Joseph and his young family left on their trip in the middle of the night.

Herod planned to hurt Jesus, but God didn't let it happen. God took care of Jesus.

_____ , God will take care of you and me, too. We may not know just how he will do it, but God will take care of us.

Questions
1. Who got angry when the wise men didn't come back? (Herod)
2. What did the angel tell Joseph to do? (Take Jesus and Mary to Egypt to get away from Herod)
3. Who took care of Jesus and kept him safe? (His Father, God)

Activities
1. Say Genesis 50:24 together: "God will take care of you."
2. Write those words from Genesis 50:24 on a piece of paper, replacing *you* with your child's name. (Let him print his own name if he can.)

Prayer
Dear God, I believe you love me and will take care of me. Thank you very much. Amen.

THE BOY TEACHER
Luke 2:46, 47

I have made known to you everything I heard from my Father.
John 15:15

_____ , have Mom and Dad ever wondered where you were? Perhaps they looked for you in the house and all around the yard. Maybe they called your friend's house. No matter where they looked, they couldn't find you.

One time when Jesus was twelve years old, Mary and Joseph couldn't find him. They looked for three long days. Finally, they went to the temple.

"There he is!" said Mary. "He's over there with the teachers."

Twelve-year-old Jesus was sitting and talking with the teachers. But a strange thing was happening. Not only were the teachers teaching Jesus, but Jesus was teaching *them*. Everyone who heard him was surprised at how much Jesus knew about God. They didn't know that Jesus was God's Son. They didn't know that Jesus had been in Heaven with God before he came to earth. And Jesus loved talking about his Father, God.

Questions
1. Where did Mary and Joseph find Jesus? (In the temple, talking with the teachers)
2. Why were the teachers surprised? (Jesus knew so much.)
3. Who loved to talk about his Father, God? (Jesus)

Activities
1. Count to twelve, Jesus' age at this time.
2. Ask your child to teach you something he has learned recently.

Prayer
Dear God, I know that Jesus is your Son. I know that everything Jesus said is the truth from you. I'll listen to what the Bible says about Jesus. Amen.

JESUS GROWS UP
Luke 2:46-52

Jesus continued to learn more and more and to grow physically.
People liked him, and he pleased God. *Luke 2:52*

_____ , do you remember where Mary and Joseph found Jesus? Yes, they found him in the temple-church, talking with the teachers. He surprised the teachers by answering lots of questions about God.

Mary was happy to find Jesus. "Jesus, we didn't know *where* you were!" she said. "We've been looking all over."

"Didn't you know that I'd be in my Father's house, doing his work?" asked Jesus. "Why didn't you look for me here first? I need to be where my Father's work is."

Mary and Joseph didn't really understand what Jesus was saying, even though they knew Jesus was God's Son. Perhaps this was the first time Jesus had talked about it.

So Jesus went back home with Mary and Joseph and always obeyed them. Every day, Jesus learned more. Every day, Jesus grew bigger. He had many friends, and he was kind to everyone. And every day, Jesus pleased God his Father.

Questions

1. Who said, "I need to be where my Father's work is?" (Jesus)
2. Where did Jesus go after Mary and Joseph found him? (Back home with them)
3. Who was kind to everyone and had many friends? (Jesus)

Activities
Make a print or tracing of your child's hand on a piece of paper. Save it to compare with your child's hand size next year.

Prayer
Dear God, help me to grow up to be wise and kind like Jesus.

MAKING ROOM FOR JESUS
Matthew 3:7-12; Luke 3:3-14

I stand at the door and knock. If anyone hears my voice and opens the door, I will come in. *Revelation 3:20*

_____ , many people came to see and hear John the Baptist. Temple leaders came. Soldiers came. City leaders came. Even mothers, fathers, and children came to see and hear this man who wore funny clothes. "Get ready," John said. "Make room for Jesus in your hearts and lives."

Some people understood and believed John's words. But others thought they didn't need to make room for Jesus. They thought all their rules were enough to please God. "Abraham is our great-great grandfather," they said. "He was OK. We must be OK, too."

"Just because you follow a lot of rules doesn't mean you know God," said John. "God wants each person to make room for Jesus."

_____ , God sent Jesus. And he wants every person, even children, to make room in his life for Jesus. We can make room in our lives for Jesus by deciding to believe, pray, and love. Going to church and learning stories from the Bible will help us when we decide to make room for Jesus.

Questions
1. Who came to see John? (Church leaders, soldiers, dads, moms, and children)
2. Whom did John say needed to get ready for Jesus? (All people)

Activity
Count the soldiers in the picture. Count the children. Point to John.

Prayer
Dear God, I know that just because I go to church, it doesn't mean that I know God. I want to open up my heart to make room for Jesus. Amen.

WHAT'S YOUR NAME?
Matthew 3:1-12; Mark 1:7, 8; Luke 3:15-18

The Lord looks at the heart. *1 Samuel 16:7*

What's your whole name? (Pause for answer.) You want people to call you by your right name, don't you, _____ ? So do I. I don't want to be called by my sister's, brother's, or friend's name.

John the Baptist wanted to be called by his right name, too. But some people thought he might be the Christ, a name that means "God's chosen one."

"That's not my name," said John. "I'm not the Christ. I'm John. God promised to send someone special, but my job is to tell you about him. He is God's Son. He knows everything. When he comes, he will know who really believes in him. I want to help get you ready for God's chosen one. Will you be ready to believe in him when he comes?"

Messiah is a name that means the same thing as *Christ*. God had promised to send the Messiah. And he kept his promise when he sent Jesus to earth. Jesus Christ is like no other man. He can see inside us, so he knows how we really feel and think. He knows and loves us more than anyone else does. This is great news.

Questions
1. What were some of the people calling John? (They thought he was the Christ.)
2. What did John say? ("No, I'm not the Christ.")

Activities
1. Say your whole name.
2. Write your name on a piece of paper. Draw a picture of yourself on that page.

Prayer
Dear Jesus, you can see inside my heart. You know how I really think and feel. It feels good to have you know all about me. Amen.

GOD'S PROMISE
Isaiah 11:1-5; Matthew 3:16

The Spirit of the Lord will rest upon that king. Isaiah 11:2

A long time ago, long before Jesus was born, God promised that someone special would one day come to earth. We can read those promises in the Old Testament of our Bible.

Some people believed God. They watched and waited. Finally the day came. John the Baptist said, "He's here. God's special one is here." This news made the waiting people happy. We can read about Jesus in the New Testament of our Bible.

Years before Jesus was born, God said, "My Spirit will be on this one. He'll obey me. He'll be wise and kind. He'll be fair to all people." The believing and waiting people remembered these words of God. So when the Spirit of God came on Jesus the day John baptized him, they knew that Jesus was God's special one.

Sometimes we have to wait, but God's promises will always come true. These people waited for Jesus for many years. God promised the special one would come. And he did.

_____ , Jesus is God's special one.

Questions
1. Who said, "A special one will come?" (God)
2. Who is God's special one? (Jesus)
3. Do God's words come true? (Yes)

Activities
1. Fold your hands to look like a book. Pretend to read God's promises about Jesus in the Old Testament.
2. Show your child the Old and New Testaments in your Bible.

Prayer
Dear God, I believe that Jesus is the special one you promised would come. Amen.

JESUS KNOWS ALL ABOUT YOU
John 1:43-51

Lord, . . . you know all about me. *Psalm 139:1*

_____ , two brothers named Andrew and Simon met Jesus and became his special helper-friends. Still Jesus needed more helpers. So Jesus met another man named Philip. "Follow me and be my friend," said Jesus. So Philip followed Jesus.

Philip had a friend named Nathanael. Philip said, "Nathanael, remember how Moses wrote that a special man of God would come someday. Well, I've found him. He's from Nazareth. "

"You're kidding," said Nathanael. "How can anyone good come from that bad city?"

"See for yourself, Nathanael," answered Philip. So Nathanael followed Philip to Jesus.

"I saw you when you were far away, sitting under a tree, Nathanael," said Jesus. "Even before your friend Philip told me about you, I knew about you."

This surprised Nathanael. "You must be God's Son," he said. "Only he would know what you know. You must be the true king of Israel — the one we've been waiting for."

Jesus knew all about Nathanael before they met. Jesus knows all about you and me, too.

Questions
1. Whom did Philip invite to see Jesus? (Nathanael)
2. Who knew about Nathanael even before they met? (Jesus)
3. Who said to Jesus, "You must be God's Son." (Nathanael)

Activities
1. Draw a picture of Nathanael sitting under the tree before he went to see Jesus.
2. Read Psalm 139:1 aloud.

Prayer
Dear Jesus, you know everything. You knew about Nathanael, and you know all about me. Thanks. Amen.

A SPECIAL PLACE
John 2:12-16

My Temple will be called a house for prayer. Isaiah 56:7

_____ , have you ever been on a trip with your family? Jesus took a trip with his family and friends. In Jerusalem, Jesus went to the temple-church. People worshiped and sang praise to God at the temple.

But this time was different. When Jesus got there, he didn't like what he saw. People who wanted to pray and sing couldn't do it, because the temple courts were full of other people yelling, "Buy my sheep! Buy my birds! Come over here. Mine are better!" Some people sat at tables trading money from different countries. None of those people was thinking about God.

"Take those things away from here!" said Jesus. "This is my Father's house. It's not a place for buying and selling!" Then Jesus made all the sellers and money-traders leave.

Jesus is God's Son. God is Jesus' Father. Jesus wanted all people to remember that God's house is a special place.

Questions
1. Who took a trip with his family and friends? (Jesus)
2. Where was the temple? (In Jerusalem)
3. What did Jesus find in the temple? (Animals, noise, money)
4. What did Jesus say to the sellers and money-traders? ("Take those things away from here. This is my Father's house.")

Activities
1. Draw a picture of the temple with animals, loud people, and money-traders.
2. Draw another picture of the temple with people praying and singing to God.

Prayer
Dear God, Jesus said that your temple-church was a special place. Help me to remember that my church is the special place where I go to learn and sing about you. Amen.

THE BEST FRIEND OF ALL
John 3:22-30

He [Jesus] must become greater. *John 3:30*

"Hey, John," said John's friends. "This man named Jesus is baptizing people in the river. And people are going to see him and not coming to you anymore."

"Great," answered John, "that means I've done what God asked me to do. That makes me happy. I've been busy telling people about Jesus. Now that he's here, my job is almost over. Jesus will be more help to people than I ever was."

Like John, when we do our job, the job God wants us to do, we don't have to be jealous of anyone else. What are some examples of what our work might be? (*Obeying parents, sharing toys, going to school, helping with chores.*) Jesus did not do John's job, and John did not do Jesus' work. We each have our own work to do.

_____ , we can invite a friend to believe and love Jesus. But when that friend believes in Jesus, then Jesus becomes his most important friend. We can love and help a friend, but Jesus is the best friend of all.

Questions
1. Who was happy that people were going to Jesus? (John)
2. Who is the best friend of all? (Jesus)

Activities
1. Name your friends.
2. Draw a picture of Jesus and John with their arms around each other.

Prayer
Dear Jesus, I want to tell my friend about you. I know that you are the most important person in my friend's life. Amen.

A SPECIAL DRINK
John 4:1-30

The water I give will become a spring of water flowing inside him.
It will give him eternal life. *John 4:14*

The Jews and the Samaritans did not usually like one another. But Jesus was different. He loved all people, no matter where they lived and what they looked like.

One day in Samaria, Jesus got tired. He sat down by a water well to rest.

While Jesus rested, a Samaritan woman came to get some water from the well. "May I have a drink, please?" Jesus asked the woman.

"You're asking me?" said the woman. "I thought you Jews didn't like us Samaritans."

"You don't know who I am, do you?" said Jesus. "If you knew me, you'd ask me to give you a special kind of living water. This living water is better than anything else. "

"What's this special kind of water you're talking about, sir?" asked the woman.

"You must get a drink of water from this well each day or you get very thirsty," Jesus said. "The water I'm talking about is different. It comes from inside you — when you decide to believe in the Son of God."

"I know that someday God will send someone special to help us," said the woman.

"I'm that one," said Jesus. Then the woman went back into town. She told everyone that she had talked to Jesus and become his friend. Many people in the town became Jesus' friends, too.

Questions
1. Who sat down by the well to rest? (Jesus)
2. Did the woman become Jesus' friend? (Yes)

Activity
Drink a cup of cool, refreshing water.

Prayer
Dear God, water helps my thirsty throat. But Jesus' special water helps my thirsty heart. Thank you for helping my thirsty heart. I love you. Amen.

JESUS IS GOD'S SON
John 5:19-26

Whoever hears what I say and believes in the One who sent me has eternal life. John 5:24

Jesus and his Father were together in Heaven when they made the world. Then at just the right time, God sent Jesus to earth to show all people (even you and me) what God is like. Anyone who believes in Jesus can know God and have eternal life. Eternal life means to live with God for always.

_____ , have you ever wondered how Jesus could do all the wonderful and special things he did while he was here on earth? It's true that Jesus walked around just like you and me. He ran down the road and past the trees. Maybe he stopped to pick flowers or cool his feet in a stream. He ate and slept just like us.

But Jesus was different. He was a man, but he was also God. But many people did not understand this.

"How can you do all these great things?" people asked.

"I'm telling you the truth, you really can believe me," answered Jesus. "It's God who tells me what to do. It's God who tells me what to say. I'm God's Son. He's my Father. If you believe in me and listen to me, then you can know God, too. And you can live with God for always."

Questions
1. Did Jesus live on earth like us? (Yes)
2. Who told Jesus what to do and say? (God)
3. How can we know God? (By believing in Jesus and listening to him.)

Activities
1. Pretend to take a walk with Jesus and name some of the things you might see together. (Ideas: clouds, birds, puppies, butterflies, stones, grass.)
2. Draw a picture of Jesus walking down the road, picking flowers, or wading in the pool.

Prayer
Dear Jesus, I believe that your words are true. I believe you are God's Son. Amen.

BETTER THAN A SUPER-HERO
Mark 1:21-28

God is greater than we are! *Job 33:12*

_____ , have you ever dressed up like a super-hero? It's fun to make believe you can do anything, isn't it? But remember that super-heroes are not real, and no one is as powerful as Jesus.

One day Jesus and his friends stopped at the synagogue. A synagogue was a place like a church building where people came to worship and learn about God. On this day, Jesus taught. He was a good teacher. While Jesus talked, a man with an evil spirit yelled loudly, "I know who you are! You come from God."

"Be quiet, and come out of that man," said Jesus. Then the evil spirit left the man. The man was different from that moment on.

All the people saw what Jesus did. "Who is this man named Jesus?" they asked. "He has more power than anyone else!" Jesus made the evil spirit go away. He made the man well. Jesus is better than a super-hero.

Questions
1. Where did Jesus teach? (Synagogue)
2. What is a synagogue? (A building where people meet for worship)
3. Who is better than any super-hero? (Jesus)

Activities
1. Draw a picture of a super-hero.
2. Draw a picture of Jesus. Write "Jesus is better" under the picture.

Prayer
Dear Jesus, I know you are powerful. You are better than a super-hero. I'm glad that you are my friend. Amen.

JESUS THE HELPER
Mark 1:40-45

So the news about Jesus spread. Mark 1:45

_____ , have you ever had a sore on your knee? It hurt, didn't it? Jesus met a man with a disease called leprosy. He had sores all over his body. He was so sick that he couldn't live with his family. One day the hurting man came to Jesus. "Will you make me well?" he asked. "I know you can do it."

"I'd love to make you well," said Jesus. He touched the sick man, and the man's sores went away.

Then Jesus said, "Don't tell anyone about what happened just now. Follow God's law and go show the priest first. That will help everyone believe you're really healed. Then go live with your family again."

But the man was so excited that he told everyone what Jesus had done.

Many people heard about all the kind and wonderful things Jesus did. They left their houses and their work to go and find Jesus. Jesus couldn't walk on the city streets, because people crowded around him. They wouldn't let him rest or eat or even move. Finally, Jesus had to stay outside the city. Then the people came there to see him.

Jesus was the best helper. He loved and helped people wherever he went.

Questions
1. What did the man with the sores ask Jesus to do? (Make him well)
2. Did Jesus make him well? (Yes)

Activity
Put a bandage on an "ouchie."

Prayer
Dear Jesus, thank you for loving all people, even sick people. Amen.

JESUS' SPECIAL FRIENDS
Mark 3:13-19; Luke 6:12-16

The next morning, Jesus called his followers to him.
He chose 12 of them, whom he named "apostles."
Luke 6:12, 13

One night Jesus walked by himself up a tall mountain. He wanted to be alone to talk with his Father, God. Jesus prayed all night. Maybe he talked with God about his friends. Perhaps he talked with God about the words he would teach his friends, and about the wonderful things they would do together.

The next morning Jesus called his friends to a meeting. "Thanks for coming," said Jesus. "I have big news. I've chosen twelve of you to be my special helper-friends. I'll call you 'apostles.' We'll work and teach together. You'll go with me on my trips. I'll tell you about my Father, God. We'll have good times together."

Jesus loved his helper-friends. They helped Jesus tell many people how to know God.

_____ , friends are important to us, aren't they? Jesus thought friends were important, too. Peter, John, James, and Thomas were four of Jesus' twelve helper-friends. Do you have any friends with these names?

Questions
1. Where did Jesus go one night alone? (Up the mountain to pray)
2. Who thinks that friends are important? (Jesus)

Activities
1. Name three of your child's friends. Name three of your friends.
2. Name one of Jesus' helper-friends.

Prayer
Dear God, thank you for your helper-friends. I know they helped you tell others about how to live. Please help my friends today. I care about them. Amen.

Note to parents/teachers
All twelve apostles were as follows: Simon Peter; Peter's brother, Andrew; brothers James and John; Philip, Bartholomew; Matthew; Thomas; another James; another Simon; Judas; and Judas Iscariot.

JESUS THE TEACHER
Matthew 5:1, 13-16, 43-47

Jesus taught the people. *Matthew 5:2*

_____ , do you have a favorite teacher? It's nice to listen to that teacher, isn't it? Jesus was a teacher. People liked to listen to him, just like you like to listen to your special teacher.

One day Jesus walked up a grassy hill and sat down in the middle of a big field. He called his twelve new helper-friends to him. He had lots of things to teach them. Others followed Jesus and his friends up the hill. They, too, sat on the grass and listened while Jesus taught.

Jesus said, "We don't put the kitchen light underneath a bowl, do we? No way! We put the light out in the open so everyone can see what we're doing.

"At your houses, you keep the lights on so you can see to work and play with your friends and family. In the same way, your lives can be like lights for other people. You can show them how to live in ways that please God."

Then Jesus said, "Love and pray for your neighbors. Love even the people who aren't nice to you."

Jesus was a good teacher. His important words, written in the Bible, can help us today.

Questions
1. Who taught the people? (Jesus)
2. Did people listen when he taught? (Yes)
3. Whom did Jesus tell us to love? (All people)

Activities
1. Have your child pretend to be your teacher.
2. Put a lamp or flashlight under the bed. Demonstrate that no one can see a light that's hidden.

Prayer
Dear Jesus, I want to learn from your important words in the Bible. Help me understand. Amen.

WHAT IF?
Matthew 6:25-34

He takes care of me. *Psalm 16:5*

"Mom and I are going on a little trip," said Dad. "We'll be gone for three days and two nights. Mrs. Smith will stay here at the house with you and your brother."

Rebecca liked Mrs. Smith, but . . . Mom and Dad gone for three whole days! What if it thundered? What if her little brother, Roger, got sick? What if *she* got sick? A tear ran down Rebecca's cheek.

"What's wrong, honey?" asked Dad.

"I'm afraid," said Rebecca. "What if something happens to us while you're gone?"

"Mrs. Smith will be here. You like her, don't you?"

Rebecca nodded.

"And God will help you, you know," said Dad. "He cares about the birds, and he cares about you and Roger. We'll be back again after two nights. And always remember that your mom and I love you very much."

Rebecca reached out and hugged her dad. "I'm glad God cares about Roger and me," she whispered.

_____ , God cares about you and me, too.

Questions
1. Who was going on a trip? (Rebecca's mom and dad)
2. Was Rebecca worried? (Yes)
3. Who said that God would help Rebecca and Roger? (Dad)

Activities
1. Count to three. Hold up three fingers.
2. Fill in this blank with your child's name: God cares for _____ .

Prayer
Dear God, thank you for taking care of me when I am away from my mom and dad. Amen.

Note to parents/teachers
Little children sometimes wonder whether mom or dad will come back after being away. Assure your child that Rebecca's parents came back after three days and two nights. Then assure him that you, too, will always return. Hug your child.

JESUS SURPRISES EVERYONE
Luke 7:11-17

But Christ is the power of God. 1 Corinthians 1:24

One day Jesus walked down the streets of a city called Nain. He saw lots of people crowded around a crying woman. Jesus soon learned that the sad woman's son had died. She didn't have a husband, and now she had no son. She was alone.

Jesus walked over to the sad mother. "Don't worry," he said. "Don't cry." Then he turned and said, "Young man, get up." Right away, the young man sat up and began to talk!

Jesus surprised the people. They had never seen anyone with power to make a person who had died come back to life. Jesus did what no one else could do. Because of Jesus' miracle, the people praised and thanked God.

_____ , this is a story about when Jesus was here on earth. He isn't here anymore. Now Jesus is in Heaven with his Father, God. But his power has not changed.

Jesus is the power of God. God has great power. That means

that he can do difficult things. He is strong and can make things happen. God and Jesus share the same power because Jesus is God's Son.

Jesus' power hasn't changed, and Jesus still cares about people, too.

Questions
1. Why was the woman crying? (Her son died.)
2. Who made the young man alive again? (Jesus)

Activities
1. Name the city or town where you live.
2. Take a walk down one of the streets where you live.

Prayer
Dear Jesus, you are stronger and more powerful than anyone. I know you care about me, my family, and my friends. Amen.

BABY BIRDS
Matthew 10:29, 30

So don't be afraid. You are worth much more than many birds.
Matthew 10:31

"You're not alone," Jesus taught. "Don't worry. I am with you. I know all about you. My Father, God, knows how many hairs you have on your head. He knows every bird that flies in the sky. If just one little bird falls, God knows it. You are much more important than the birds."

_____ , Jesus said these words long ago. They are written in the Bible.

Becky remembered Jesus' words as she watched a big brown bird fly back and forth in front of her bedroom window. "Mom," said Becky. "Come see what I found."

Mom hurried into Becky's room. "Talk real quiet," whispered Becky. "We don't want to scare the mommy bird."

Becky stood on her tiptoes. She pointed to the tree outside her window. "See the baby birds inside that nest?" she asked. "They're hungry. The mommy's been bringing them food. God cares about these birds, doesn't he?" said Becky. "He cares about you and me, too," said Becky.

And _____ , God cares about you, too. We can thank him for that.

Questions
1. Who knows how many hairs are on your head? (God)
2. What did Becky see outside of her window? (Birds)
3. Who cares about you and loves you? (God)

Activities
1. Try to count the hairs on your head.
2. Make a sound like hungry baby birds.

Prayer
Dear God, Jesus said that you know when one little bird falls down — and you care. I know you care about me, too. Amen.

IT'S RAINING! IT'S POURING!
Mark 4:35-41

Don't be afraid. I will help you. *Isaiah 41:10*

"It's nice out — not too hot and not too cold," said Mom. "Let's walk to the store."

"How about if I ride my bike slow next to you?" asked Matt.

"OK," said Mom. "I only need a few things. You can carry them in your bike bag."

While Matt and his mom were in the store, the weather changed. Clouds started to cover the sun.

"It looks like it might rain." said Mom. "We'd better hurry."

Then a big dark cloud rolled across the sky and stopped over their heads. And it rained! Hard! "We're getting soaked," shouted Matt. "What should we do?" Matt was worried.

Just then Matt's Sunday school teacher drove by. She slowed down. "I thought that looked like you," she said. "Climb in. I'll put Matt's bike into the truck bed and drive you home."

It's normal to be afraid when we're in trouble and don't know what to do next. That's why Jesus says, "I'll help you. Believe me and don't worry." When Jesus' friends were afraid of a storm, Jesus knew how to help. He stopped the wind. Jesus knew how to help Matt, too. He sent the Sunday school teacher. _____, Jesus knows how to help us, too. He wants us to believe he can and will help us with all our problems — big or small.

Questions
1. Who got caught in a rain storm? (Matt and his mother)
2. Who helped Matt and his mom? (Matt's Sunday school teacher)

Activity
Make a grocery list together.

Prayer
Jesus, you helped your friends in a storm. You helped Matt. I know you'll help me, too. Amen.

LET'S PRAY
Matthew 14:23; Mark 6:46

The Lord is close to everyone who prays to him. *Psalm 145:18*

_____ , let's name times when we might pray to God. Yes, we might pray at mealtime or at bedtime or just anytime we want to. Praying is an important thing to do.

Jesus thought praying was important. Often he went away to pray. He walked up by himself into the hills. This praying time was special to him.

What do you think he prayed about? Maybe he praised God. Psalm 145 says, "I will praise your greatness, my God . . . . I will praise you every day . . . . I will tell how great you are . . . . All living things look to you for food . . . . I will praise the Lord." Perhaps he asked God to help him. Psalm 143:8 says, "Show me what I should do because my prayers go up to you." Maybe Jesus prayed for his 12 helper-friends.

Jesus believed it was a good idea to spend time praying to God. If it was good for Jesus, it is good for us, too. God promises to be close to those of us who pray to him. We don't have to be in a special place to pray. We can talk to God anytime and anywhere. We can pray silently or aloud.

Questions
1. Where did Jesus go to pray? (Into the hills)
2. Whom did Jesus talk to when he prayed? (His Father, God)
3. What did Jesus believe was a good idea? (To pray to God)

Activities
1. Make a short prayer list. Write five names of people you'd like to pray for and several things you are thankful for.
2. Open your Bible to the book of Psalms. Look up Psalm 145:18.

Prayer
Dear God, just like Jesus I think it's a good idea to pray to you. Thank you for _____ and _____ . Amen.

ROW, ROW, ROW YOUR BOAT
Mark 6:45-52; John 6:16-21

Don't be afraid. It is I. *John 6:20*

After the big picnic, Jesus' friends walked down the hill to Lake Galilee. They got into a boat and tried to row across the lake. But the wind was blowing too hard against them.

Then Jesus' friends looked up and saw a man walking to them on the water! "Who is that?" they said. "Is it a ghost?"

"Don't be afraid. It is I," said the man. They knew right away that it was Jesus.

"Boy, we're glad to see you!" they said. Jesus got into the boat, and then the wind stopped.

Jesus' friends were amazed. _____ , only Jesus could walk on water. Anyone else would sink. But Jesus made the water. And Jesus has power to do anything.

_____ , we don't need to be afraid when he helps us.

Questions
1. Where did Jesus' friends go? (In a boat on Lake Galilee)
2. What splashed into the boat? (Waves splashed water into the boat)
3. Who walked to them on the water? (Jesus)
4. Were Jesus' friends glad to see him? (Yes)

Activities
1. Pretend the sofa, bed, or chair is a boat. Sit on your feet and pretend to row the "boat" on a windy sea.
2. Sing "Row, Row, Row Your Boat."

Prayer
Dear Jesus, you walked on the water. You can do anything. I will believe you and not be afraid. Amen.

HEARING, TALKING, SHARING
Mark 7:31-37

Jesus does everything well. Mark 7:37

_____ , it would be hard if you couldn't hear me reading to you, wouldn't it? (Pause for a response.) A long time ago there was a man who couldn't hear or talk. But he had friends. The friends came to Jesus and said, "Please touch our friend and make him hear and talk."

So Jesus took this man on a walk with just the two of them. He put his fingers in the man's ears and touched the man's tongue. He looked up to Heaven like he was praying to his Father. "Be opened!" Jesus said. He was telling the part of the man's body that didn't work right to open up and start working. And do you know what happened?

Right away the man could hear. He heard his friends talking to him and he answered back. It was great! All the people said, "Everything Jesus does is good. He can do anything."

Questions
1. Who asked Jesus to help the man who couldn't hear or talk? (His friends)
2. Who touched the man's ears and tongue? (Jesus)

Activities
1. Cover your ears and pretend that you can't hear.
2. Discuss how it would be if you couldn't hear. (Ideas: If you couldn't hear words, it would be hard to say words correctly. You couldn't hear when a car came down the street.)
3. Sometimes people with hearing impairments talk with their hands. Each sign they make with their hands stands for a letter of the alphabet or a word. You and your child may wish to go to the library to get a book about "signing."

Prayer
Dear Jesus, I know that everything you and your Father do is good. I want to share your goodness with my friends. Amen.

FEEDING THE HUNGRY
Mark 8:1-10

He [Jesus] said, "I feel sorry for these people." *Mark 8:1, 2*

_____ , what does it feel like when you're hungry? Sometimes your stomach hurts and you want to eat, right? You want that hungry feeling to go away.

One day more than four thousand people crowded around Jesus. They listened to him teach for a long time. "I feel sorry for them," said Jesus. "They don't have food to eat. If they start walking home now, they might be too weak to get all the way home."

"But we can't feed all these people," said Jesus' friends.

"Well," said Jesus, "how many loaves of bread do you have?"

"Seven," they answered. So Jesus decided to have a big picnic.

"Everyone, sit down on the ground," said Jesus. Then he prayed, "Thank you, Father, for this food." Jesus' friends gave out bread to all the men, women, and children. The people ate until they weren't hungry anymore. With just seven loaves of bread, Jesus made enough food for everyone. Jesus loved and cared for the hungry people. He did something no one else could do.

Questions
1. How many people were listening to Jesus teach? (More than four thousand)
2. What did these people need? (Food)
3. How many loaves of bread did they have? (Seven)
4. Who fed all the people? (Jesus)

Activities
1. Talk about thanking God before you eat each meal.
2. Make up a table prayer to say together.

Prayer
Dear God, thank you for the food you help our family get. Amen.

WALKING TREES
Mark 8:22-26

He takes care of me. Psalm 16:5

Jesus did many wonderful things. He helped people. He cared about moms and dads and boys and girls. He made sick people well. Jesus spent lots of time with his twelve special friends.

One time Jesus and his friends went to a city called Bethsaida. Some people came up to talk. They brought their blind friend with them. "Jesus, touch our friend," they said. "Please make him see again."

Jesus put his hands on the man. "Can you see now?" he asked.

The man lifted his head and looked around. "Yes," he said. "I see people walking around, but they look like trees." So Jesus put his hands on the man's eyes again. When the man opened his eyes, he looked up and down and all around. He could see! His friends didn't look like trees anymore!

Sometimes Jesus may help us in a different way than he helps our friend. This is OK. We can trust Jesus to do the right thing. _____ , Jesus cared about the blind man and helped him. And Jesus cares about you, too.

Questions
1. What is the name of the city where Jesus and his friends went? (Bethsaida)
2. Who needed Jesus' help? (The blind man and his friends)
3. What does being blind mean? (Not being able to see)
4. Who cared about the blind man and made him see again? (Jesus)

Activity
Close your eyes (or put on a blindfold). Try to write your name or draw a picture.

Prayer
Dear Jesus, you cared about the blind man. You care about me, too. Thank you. Amen.

THE BEST PROMISE
Mark 8:27-30

You are the Christ. Mark 8:29

_____ , Jesus and his twelve helpers spent many days and months together. Jesus told his helpers things that he didn't tell anyone else. One day he and his helper-friends went on a trip together. While they were traveling, Jesus turned to his friends and asked, "Who do people think I am? What do they say about me?"

"Well, some say that you are John the Baptist," they answered, "Others say you are Elijah." Elijah was a man who lived a long time before Jesus was born. Elijah was a prophet. He told people about God. "But other people say you are a new prophet of God," they said.

"Who do you think I am?" asked Jesus.

"You are the Christ," said Peter. Peter knew that Jesus was from God. Many years before Peter was born, God promised to send a special person who would be called the Christ, or Messiah. Jesus was that special one. Jesus was happy that Peter knew who he really was.

Questions
1. Who spent many days and months together? (Jesus and his twelve helpers)
2. Who did people say Jesus was? (John the Baptist, Elijah, a new prophet)
3. Who did Peter say Jesus was? (The Christ, or Messiah; the special one God promised to send)

Activity
Draw a picture of Jesus talking to his twelve special friends.

Prayer:
Dear Jesus, I believe, like Peter, that you are the special one God promised would come. Amen.

THE SHEPHERD KNOWS MY NAME
John 10:1-18

I am the good shepherd. *John 10:14*

_____ , what sound does a sheep make? Yes, a sheep says baaa. A shepherd is someone who takes care of a flock of sheep. A flock is a group of sheep who live, eat, and play together. Listen to a story about a mother sheep named Woolly and her little lamb named Cuddly.

One day Woolly and Cuddly walked together in the field. Their sheep friends stayed in the field, eating juicy green grass. But Woolly and Cuddly were having so much fun that they didn't watch where they were going. They went further and further away from the rest of the sheep. They headed straight for trouble. A few more steps and they would fall down a hill.

Just then the shepherd saw them. "Woolly, Cuddly," he called loudly. Right away the mommy and baby lamb heard their shepherd's voice. They turned and headed back to the safety of the shepherd's care. The good shepherd saved them from trouble.

Jesus is *our* good shepherd. We are his little sheep and lambs. He knows my name and he knows *your* name. Like the loving shepherd, he helps us when we need help.

Questions
1. Who walked away from the other sheep? (The mommy sheep and baby lamb)
2. What were their names? (Woolly and Cuddly)
3. Who helped the sheep stay away from trouble? (The shepherd)
4. Who is *our* good shepherd? (Jesus)

Activities
1. Make sheep sounds together.
2. Draw a picture of a little lamb and cover it with cotton balls for wool.

Prayer
Dear Jesus, you're my good shepherd. I'm your little lamb. I know that you know my name. Thank you for watching over me. Amen.

SOME DO; SOME DON'T
John 7:10-31

But many of the people believed in Jesus. *John 7:31*

People in Jerusalem were talking about Jesus and looking for him. Some of the people said Jesus was a good man. Others weren't sure.

Then Jesus came to the temple-church to teach. Jesus was a good teacher. The people who heard him were amazed at everything Jesus knew about God. Some said, "This man didn't study in our school. How come he knows so much?"

Jesus said, "I come from God. He's my Father. Every word I teach you is from God. The God you've always worshiped is the same God who sent me."

Some people said, "We know God promised to send a special one someday. Could Jesus be this man?"

Jesus heard the people's questions. "Yes, I am that man," he answered. "God sent me."

Some of the people believed Jesus. Some didn't. This happened a long time ago. It is still like that today. Some people believe Jesus' words and some don't.

_____ , Jesus' words are written in the Bible. It's a good decision to believe Jesus.

Questions
1. Who is Jesus' Father? (God)
2. Where did Jesus come from? (God)
3. What is the same today as when Jesus taught long ago? (Some believe; some don't.)

Activity
Ask your child to "teach" you a Bible story.

Prayer
Dear Jesus, some people believe in you and some people don't. I have decided to believe in you. And I'm glad. Amen.

LET'S GET HIM!
John 7:32-53

So the people did not agree with each other about Jesus. *John 7:43*

 _____ , what do you think the people said about Jesus' teaching? *(Pause for a response. Any answer is fine.)* Some said, "That's good teaching. I believe it." Others said, "He's trying to fool us. He's not from God."

Some of the people's leaders wanted to hurt Jesus. Some even wanted to kill him. Everywhere the leaders went, they heard people talking about Jesus. They were jealous. They were afraid the people would listen to Jesus and not to them. "Let's get him!" they said.

But Jesus got away. "I'm going to be here and teach you a little while longer," Jesus said. "Then I'm going back to God. Remember, God's the one who sent me here."

The leaders didn't understand Jesus. And they all had different ideas about what Jesus said. They tried to figure it all out, but they chose not to believe what Jesus said about himself. So they just gave up trying to talk about it at all and went home.

Questions
1. Who were the people whispering about? (Jesus)
2. What did the leaders want to do? (Hurt or kill Jesus)
3. Where did the leaders go when they could not agree about Jesus? (Home)

Activity
Name some of the ways you might feel when someone doesn't like you or wants to hurt you. (Ideas: sad, alone, scared, mad)

Prayer
Dear Jesus, you must have been sad when the leaders didn't believe you and wanted to kill you. You loved and taught them anyway because God wanted you to. Thanks for obeying your Father. Amen.

LEARNING TO SHARE
Luke 12:13-21

A greedy person causes trouble. *Proverbs 28:25*

"Jesus, tell my brother to share with me," said a man standing near Jesus. "He has more than I have. Tell him to share what Dad gave him."

"I can't decide for the two of you," said Jesus. "Brothers need to talk to each other. Work it out together. Make up your own minds to share."

Then Jesus said to all the people, "Be careful not to be selfish," he said. "How many things you have doesn't make you important."

_____ , it is fun to have toys and new clothes, isn't it?

A person who doesn't share and who wants to keep all the best toys for himself is greedy. Selfish men and women or boys and girls can cause trouble among their friends and family. It is nice to have a new tricycle or video game. But Jesus said that it's even better to know and love God. When we know and love God, we want to be kind and share.

Questions
1. What were the brothers fighting about? (Sharing)
2. Does it make us more important if we have the most toys? (No)
3. What is better than having many things? (Knowing and loving God)

Activity
Choose one toy to share today (with a brother, sister, or friend).

Prayer
Dear God, thank you for the things I have. I'm learning that it is better to know and love you than to have lots of toys and clothes. Because I love you, I can learn to share with others. Amen.

DOING GOOD EVERY DAY
Luke 13:10-17

The people were happy for the wonderful things Jesus was doing.
Luke 13:17

When Jesus was on earth, the special day to worship God was called the Sabbath. God's law said there should be no work on the Sabbath. Some people had made many rules about what could and could not be done on the Sabbath.

One Sabbath when Jesus was teaching in a synagogue, a woman with an evil spirit came in. This woman was bent over. She had not been able to stand up straight for eighteen years.

Jesus saw her pain and cared. He said, "I'll make your back straight. Your sickness will go away."

Right away the woman stood up straight. "How good God is to make me well!" she said.

But the leader of the synagogue was angry. "It is work to heal someone," he said. "No more healing on the Sabbath."

Jesus heard him. "It isn't wrong to do good on the Sabbath day," said Jesus.

_____ , the leader cared more about the "no-work" rule than he did about people. But Jesus cared about the woman.

Questions
1. Who taught in the synagogue? (Jesus)
2. Did Jesus make the sick woman's back straight? (Yes)
3. Who was mad because Jesus made the woman well on the Sabbath day? (The synagogue leader)
4. Was it wrong to do good things on the Sabbath day? (No)

Activities
1. Bend over and walk around the room.
2. Name things that we do on Sunday, our special day to worship God.

Prayer
Dear Jesus, thank you for doing good and wonderful things every day. Amen.

YOU'RE SPECIAL!
Matthew 19:13-15

You have known the Holy Scriptures since you were a child.
2 Timothy 3:15

"Mommy, can I read the story tonight?" asked Annette as she climbed into bed. "I can 'member the words." Four-year-old Annette picked out a story about Jesus and the children. She remembered the story because she had heard her mother read it many times.

"See the children in the picture, Mom?" asked Annette. "They want Jesus to hug and pray with them. They got sad when Jesus' friends told them to go away and leave Jesus alone, 'cause he's too busy. But Jesus said, 'Let those children come see me. They are special. And I love each little one.' Jesus changed the children's sad faces to happy faces."

Annette closed the book. "Thanks for reading me a story, honey," said her mom. She leaned over and kissed Annette goodnight. "You *are* special to Jesus and to me."

_____ , you're special, too. To Jesus and to me!

Questions
1. Who read a bedtime story? (Annette)
2. What did Jesus say? ("Let those children come see me. They are special.")

Activities
1. Give your child a kiss.
2. Fold your hands like a book and pretend to read a story.

Prayer
Dear Jesus, all children are special to you. That means I'm special, too. Thank you. Amen.

THE THANK-YOU FRIENDS
Luke 17:11-19

Give thanks. *1 Thessalonians 5:18*

"Mrs. Webster, may we use your water hose?" asked Joey and Chris. "We want to run through the sprinkler."

"OK," said Mrs. Webster. "I'll help you pull the hose to Joey's yard." Joey lived next door and Chris lived across the street.

Joey and Chris ran back and forth through the sprinkler. When they finished, they turned off the faucet, rolled up the hose, and took it back to Mrs. Webster's house.

The next day Mrs. Webster's doorbell rang. When she opened her front door, there stood Joey and Chris.

"Here's something for you," said Chris. "I wrote the note and Joey drew the picture."

The note said, "Thanks for letting Joe and me use your hose. It was so much fun! You are the nicest neighbor. Sincerely, Joe and Chris."

"What a nice surprise," said Mrs. Webster. "I'll keep your note with my important papers."

Saying thank-you is a very important thing to do.

One day as Jesus walked along a road, he saw ten very sick men. "Please help us!" called the men.

"I will," said Jesus. He healed all ten men, but only one remembered to say thank-you.

_____ , Jesus was glad when the man said thank-you. He wants us to say thank-you, too.

Questions
1. Who played in the water sprinkler? (Joey and Chris)
2. How many men thanked Jesus? (Only one man)

Activity
Thank the person who read you this story.

Prayer
Dear God, help me to remember to say thank-you for all the good things that happen to me. Amen.

THE CHILDREN'S FRIEND
Matthew 19:13-15

Let the little children come to me. Matthew 19:14

"Let's take the children to see Jesus today," said one mother to another. Then that mother told another mother. And that mother told another mother. Soon all the parents in the neighborhood planned to take their children to see Jesus. Moms and dads liked to bring their boys and girls to Jesus, because he hugged them, told them stories, and prayed for them.

When Jesus' helpers saw the moms and dads coming over the hill with their children, they ran to meet them. "Stop," the helpers said. "Jesus is too busy. Don't bother him."

"Wait a minute," said Jesus. "Don't stop them. Let the children come on over. These little ones are precious. Grown-ups need to learn to be like these trusting children."

Jesus thought the children were special. He blessed the boys and girls who came to see him. He prayed to his Father God about the children.

_____ , Jesus loves *all* little children. Jesus is the children's friend.

Questions
1. Who wanted to bring the children to see Jesus? (The parents)
2. Who said Jesus was too busy to see the children? (Jesus' helpers)
3. Did Jesus want to see the children? (Yes)

Activities
1. Sing "Jesus Loves Me, This I Know."
2. Give your child a hug.
3. Name some things you think Jesus prayed about when he blessed the children.

Prayer
Dear Jesus, thank you for loving all children. Thank you for loving me. Amen.

ASKING FOR HELP
Mark 10:46-52

What do you want me to do for you? *Mark 10:51*

_____ , what do you think it would be like if you couldn't see? *(Pause for a response. Any response is fine.)* One day, Jesus and his friends walked by a man who couldn't see. The blind man sat by the roadside. "Jesus," said the man, "please help me!"

"Shhh! Don't bother Jesus. He's busy," said the many people who followed Jesus.

But the man spoke louder. "Jesus, please help me!"

So Jesus stopped what he was doing. "Tell that man to come here," he said.

"Hey, cheer up!" the people said. "Jesus wants to see you." The man hurried to Jesus.

"What do you want me to do for you?" Jesus asked.

The man knew he couldn't help himself. So when Jesus asked him, the blind man was honest. He said, "I want to see."

"OK," said Jesus. "You asked for my help. You believed in me. You'll no longer be without your sight." Right away the man could see. And he followed Jesus.

Questions
1. Who asked, "What do you want me to do for you?" (Jesus)
2. What did the man want? (To see again)
3. Did the man get what he wanted from Jesus? (Yes)

Activity
Jesus helped the man. Name times that you might need help from Jesus. (Ideas: sharing, obeying, going to sleep at night, telling the truth.)

Prayer
Dear Jesus, the man knew he needed your help. Help me to know when I need your help, too. Amen.

WHAT'S GOING ON?
Matthew 26:6-13; Mark 14:3-9; John 12:1-8

She did a very beautiful thing for me. *Matthew 26:10*

_____ , do you like to have dinner with friends? It's nice to do sometimes, isn't it? One evening, Jesus ate dinner with some of his friends. The dinner was at Simon's home. Mary and Martha and their brother Lazarus were there, too.

While everyone else ate, Mary brought in a bottle of very expensive perfume and poured it on Jesus' feet. Then she dried his feet with her long hair. The wonderful perfume smell filled the whole house.

The people stared at Mary. They stared at Jesus. They wondered what was going on.

Then Judas spoke up. "This perfume cost a lot of money. We could have sold it and given all the money to the poor people." (Judas didn't really care about the poor. He had been stealing money from the poor people. He only wanted the money for himself.)

Jesus said, "Don't bother Mary. She believes the things I say. Her kind deed shows how much she cares about what happens to me. You can give money to the poor after I've gone."

Mary did a kind and loving thing for Jesus.

Questions
1. Who was at the dinner? (Simon, Lazarus, Mary, Martha, Jesus)
2. Who put perfume on Jesus? (Mary)

Activity
Carefully open a bottle of perfume or cologne. Sniff it. Discuss how the aroma fills the room.

Prayer
Dear Jesus, Mary loved you. She believed all the things you said. I love you, too. Help me to always believe your words and to do kind things to please you. Amen.

Note to parents/teachers
In Jesus' time, when a person died, perfumed ointments were placed on the body. Mary was preparing Jesus' body for his coming death.

CAN ROCKS SING?
Mark 11:7-10; Luke 19:35-40

If my followers don't say these things, then the stones will cry out.
Luke 19:40

"Here's the donkey colt you asked for," said Jesus' friends. Jesus climbed onto the colt's back. People took off their coats and put them in the road. Others cut branches off the palm trees and put them on the ground. It was like nice carpet for Jesus to ride on.

"How wonderful Jesus is!" the people shouted. "He makes blind people see. He loves children. He's the special one God promised to send."

But some people didn't sing. They weren't happy. "Jesus, tell these people to stop singing and be quiet," they said.

"I can't do that," said Jesus. "They're praising God. And if they don't praise God, the rocks and stones will start to sing."

_____ , it's good to praise God!

Questions
1. What did Jesus ride? (A donkey colt)
2. Who put coats and palm branches on the ground? (The people)

Activities
1. Sing a song to God. (If you don't know one, make one up using the people's words in this story.)
2. Go on a walk together to collect stones and branches.
3. Find a picture of a palm tree. In Jesus' day, people waved palm branches to celebrate happy times. We remember and celebrate this special day on "Palm Sunday," one week before Easter.

Prayer
Dear Jesus, I'll keep using my voice to sing and praise you. Amen.

A TRICK QUESTION
Matthew 22:15-22; Mark 12:13-17; Luke 20:20-26

Give to Caesar the things that are Caesar's.
And give to God the things that are God's. *Matthew 22:21*

Some people tried to trick Jesus. They wanted him to do or say something wrong. One day they came to Jesus with a trick question. "Is it all right to pay taxes to Caesar?" they asked. (Caesar was the Roman leader of the government.) Jesus knew they were asking this question to try to trick him.

"Why are you trying to trick me?" he asked. "Show me the coin you use to pay the tax." The people showed him a silver coin.

"Now tell me whose picture is on this coin," said Jesus.

"Caesar's picture is on the coin," they said.

"Then give to Caesar the money and things that are his, and give to God the things that are God's."

Jesus' answer surprised the men. They said nothing and walked away.

These men wanted Jesus to give an answer that would get him in trouble with the government. But Jesus was wise. He said, "Yes, we must pay taxes to our government. But we also need to give God what he wants." _____ , God wants our love and our trust in him.

Questions
1. Why did people try to trick Jesus? (To get him in trouble with the government)
2. Did Jesus know what they were trying to do? (Yes)

Activity
Look at a U.S. coin. What does it say? ("In God We Trust." It also has a picture of someone in our country or government.)

Prayer
Dear God, we'll give you our love and trust. We'll also give our country what is right. This is what you want us to do. Amen

SAD AND GLAD DECISIONS
Matthew 26:17-25; Mark 14:17-21; John 13:21-30

He who believes in the Son has eternal life. But he who does not obey the Son will never have that life. John 3:36

The Passover feast was an important time for all Jewish people. Families and friends ate a special dinner together. It reminded the Jews of how God had saved them from slavery in Egypt many years before.

Jesus and his twelve helpers sat down to eat this special dinner together. During the meal, Jesus said, "Listen, I'm telling the truth. One of you will turn against me. One of you is really not my friend."

Jesus' words made the men sad. Each one said, "Oh, Jesus, I'm not the one, am I?"

Then quietly, so not everyone could hear, Jesus said, "Here is a piece of bread. I'm going to dip it in this bowl. Then I'll give it to the man who will turn against me." Jesus handed the bread to Judas.

"It isn't me, is it?" said Judas.

"Yes, Judas, it is you," said Jesus. "Now go. Do what you're going to do."

When Judas left the room, it was a sad, dark night. Jesus' other helper-friends didn't understand about Judas. Judas had spent many days and months with Jesus. Yet he never decided to love Jesus.

_____ , we each have a choice. It is a glad day when we decide to love and follow Jesus.

Questions
1. What was the meaning of the Passover feast? (Remembering how God saved the people from slavery in Egypt)
2. Who ate dinner with Jesus? (The twelve helper-friends)
3. Who turned against Jesus? (Judas)

Activity
Draw a sad face. Then draw a glad face.

Prayer
Dear Jesus, it's sad that Judas decided not to love you. But I have decided to love you, and I'm glad. Amen.

I LOVE YOU
John 13:34 — 16:15

I have told you these things to keep you from giving up. *John 16:1*

_____ , when you love someone, you want to be with them, right? Jesus and his friends loved each other. They spent lots of time together. Jesus told them about God. Jesus taught them many things. Here are some of the things Jesus said to his friends:

"I love you. I want you to know and believe that I love you and be happy.

"Love one another. People will know you're my friends if you love each other.

"Believe me. I am the way to get to know God. The same God who made the birds, flowers, your parents, and you is my Father.

"Don't worry. I will always help you.

"There will be times when people won't believe you when you tell them about me. Sometimes they didn't believe me, either.

"I am going to leave you and go back to Heaven to live with my Father. But I will send the Holy Spirit to live in you and help you."

Jesus told his friends all of these things to help them and to give them courage. He didn't want them to give up following and loving him even though sometimes it would be hard.

Questions
1. Who said, "I love you?" (Jesus)
2. Who will always help you? (Jesus and the Holy Spirit)

Activity
Name people you like to spend time with.

Prayer
Dear Jesus, you taught your friends many things that will help me now. Thank you for sharing these truths with me.

KNOWING GOD
John 14:1-7

I am the way. . . . The only way to the Father is through me.
John 14:6

_____ , do you like to eat and talk with the people you love? It's good to talk together about things that are important to you, isn't it? At mealtime we may talk about what you learned at preschool or what you played today. We may talk about Mom or Dad's job or going to visit Grandma.

Jesus and his special friends liked to talk together about important things, too. Jesus had special things to tell them before he died. How much Jesus loved and cared about his friends!

He said, "Don't worry! Believe God. And believe me, too. I'm going to leave you now, but I promise I'll make a place ready for you. And I'll come back someday, too."

"But, Lord, we don't know where you're going," said his helper-friend, Thomas. "We don't know the way to this place you're talking about. "

"I am the way," said Jesus. "And the place is with God the Father. I am the true way to know God and the true way to have life with God forever."

Jesus said these words to his special helpers, but he tells us the same thing. We can know God by believing Jesus. Then someday we will live with Jesus and God forever.

Questions
1. What was the name of the helper who said he didn't know the way? (Thomas)
2. Who said, "I am the way?" (Jesus)

Activity
On a large sheet of paper write, "Jesus said, 'I am the way.'" Have your child try to copy the letters of the verse. Use markers or crayons.

Prayer
Dear Jesus, I believe that you are the way to know God. Amen.

FRIENDS
John 15:12-17

But now I call you friends. John 15:15

_____ , what is a friend? *(Pause. Any response is fine.)* A friend is someone you care about. You like to be with your friend. You want to be with your friend. Sometimes you help your friend, and at other times your friend helps you. You work and play together. Real friends love one another.

After Jesus and his helpers ate the Passover meal together, Jesus said, "You are my friends. We're friends because you've decided to believe and do the things I've told you to do. You are not just my helpers anymore. If you were helpers only, we wouldn't really get to know one another. It's different now that we're friends. I've told you everything God told me. I love you, and I want you to love one another."

Being friends with Jesus is special. Friends are important. We treat our friends with kindness and respect. We tell them the truth. We share with them. We want to say nice words to them. We care when a friend feels hurt, sick, or sad. We try to help, if we can. And we want to do things that make our friends happy.

Jesus is the best friend we will ever have. We can't see Jesus, but we know he cares about everything we do. We can always talk to him.

Questions
1. Do friends care about each other? (Yes)
2. Can we be friends with Jesus? (Yes)

Activities
1. Name two of your friends. What do you do with your friends?
2. Name two things you know about your friend Jesus.

Prayer
Dear Jesus, I'm happy you're my friend. You help me so many times. Help me to love all your friends. Amen.

JESUS' PRAYER FOR YOU AND ME
John 17:1-26

I am also praying for all people who will believe in me because of the teaching of these men. John 17:20

_____ , we know that Jesus prayed to God his Father many times. One night, Jesus prayed a very special prayer.

"Father, it's almost time for me to die. I've finished the job you gave me to do here. Soon I'll be back with you. You've given me good friends. I've told them about you. I pray for my friends now. I know they love you. Please keep them safe after I leave. I pray that they might be really happy. When other people don't like them because they believe in me, help them to be happy anyway.

"I also pray for all the people who will believe in me later because of the work my friends here will do. Amen."

Jesus' helper-friends heard Jesus pray for them. We know about Jesus today because of the teaching of these men. Some of them wrote books of the Bible.

_____ , we are some of the people who have believed in Jesus later. Jesus knew about us — and prayed for us — a long time before we were born.

Questions
1. Did Jesus pray to God? (Yes)
2. Whom did Jesus pray for? (His special friends and for us)

Activity
Name some people you know who are friends of Jesus, too. A long time ago, Jesus prayed for all these people, too.

Prayer
Dear Jesus, thank you for praying for me. Amen.

JUST PRETENDING
Mark 14:43-50; John 18:1-14

"He had done nothing wrong. He had never lied." Isaiah 53:9

Judas just pretended to be Jesus' friend. He ate with Jesus. He traveled with Jesus. He watched Jesus heal many people. But he didn't really love Jesus. He cared more about making money than about being Jesus' friend.

The leaders of the people were jealous of Jesus. They paid Judas some money. Then one night Judas took soldiers and guards to a garden that was one of Jesus' favorite places.

"That's him, over there," whispered Judas. "You can grab him now." The soldiers tied Jesus up and took him away. They arrested him as if he were someone bad. But Jesus had never done anything bad in his whole life.

Jesus loved Judas. But Judas didn't care. He had decided to say no to friendship with Jesus. It was a very sad night.

But _____ , it is a very happy day when you and I decide to say yes to friendship with Jesus!

Questions
1. Who just pretended to be Jesus' friend? (Judas)
2. Where did Judas take the soldiers and guards? (To find Jesus)
3. Did they treat Jesus in a nice way? (No)

Activity
Draw a picture of Jesus in the garden before the soldiers came.

Prayer
Dear God, you must have been sad when Judas just pretended to be your friend. I'm not pretending. I really want to spend time with you and get to know you better. Amen.

LYING, LOVING, FORGIVING
Matthew 26:69-75; Mark 14:66-72; Luke 54-62

Then Peter . . . cried. *Luke 22:62*

_____ , have you ever been on a camping trip on a cold night? Perhaps you got warm by standing near a campfire.

Peter warmed his cold hands and feet over a campfire the night Jesus was arrested. While he was standing by the fire, a young woman came by. "You were with Jesus, weren't you?" she asked.

"I don't know what you're talking about," said Peter. "I've never been with the man."

As Peter walked away, someone pointed at him and said, "That man was with Jesus."

But Peter said the second time, "No, you're wrong. I do not know the man. "

"We know you're one of Jesus' friends," said another man later. "You even talk like him."

"I am not," Peter lied. Just then Jesus looked at Peter from across the yard. Then Peter remembered what Jesus had told him earlier that night: "Tonight you'll say that you don't know me. You'll lie about me three times."

Peter went outside the yard and cried. He was so sorry he had lied about knowing Jesus — he had done it because he was afraid. Deep down inside, Peter really was Jesus' friend.

Questions
1. How many times did Peter lie? (Three)
2. Was Peter sorry and sad that he lied? (Yes)

Activities
1. Pretend to warm your hands by a campfire.
2. Draw a picture of a campfire.

Prayer
Dear Jesus, Peter was sorry he lied about knowing you. Sometimes I disobey and lie. But then I'm sorry, too. Thanks for loving me still, just as you loved Peter. Amen.

PILATE AND JESUS
Matthew 27:15-31; Mark 15:6-20

Pilate let Barabbas go free and gave Jesus to them to be killed.
Luke 23:25

_____ , did Jesus ever do anything wrong? No, he never did. Jesus is the only person who never sinned.

But the leaders who were jealous of Jesus wanted to find something wrong with him. They didn't like Jesus. They wanted to kill him.

After Jesus was arrested, he was taken to the governor. His name was Pilate. Pilate could decide to let the leaders kill Jesus, or he could make them let Jesus go. The angry Jews wanted a robber and murderer named Barabbas to go free instead of Jesus.

"Why do you want to kill this man called Jesus?" asked Pilate. "I can't find anything wrong with him."

Still the people yelled, "Kill him. Put him on a cross to die."

Then Pilate saw that the people were getting loud and wild. He didn't want the people making trouble for him. He didn't really care about doing the right thing. So he gave Jesus back to the jealous and angry people.

Pilate needed to decide, and he made a bad choice. We can make a good choice, though. We can decide to love Jesus.

Questions
1. Who never did anything wrong? (Jesus)
2. Who was the governor? (Pilate)
3. Could Pilate find anything wrong with Jesus? (No)

Activity
Name the governor of the state where you live.

Prayer
Dear Jesus, Pilate decided to give you back to the angry people. He didn't care about you, but I do. I want to make good decisions. Please help me. Amen.

ANYONE CAN BE JESUS' FRIEND
Luke 23:39-43

Jesus said, "Today you will be with me in paradise!" *Luke 23:43*

Sometimes it's surprising who decides to become Jesus' friend. It may be easy for us to understand how good people can be Jesus' friends. But what about people who do bad things, like stealing and killing? Can these people be Jesus' friends, too?

Yes, anyone can decide to believe in Jesus and become his friend. Jesus can change the way a person thinks and acts.

On the day Jesus died, two other men were nailed on a cross also. These men were thieves. They had taken things that didn't belong to them. They had disobeyed the law of their country. They were supposed to die on a cross like Jesus.

One thief made fun of Jesus. But the other man said, "Hey, man, don't you get it? We've done lots of bad things. We need to be punished. But Jesus never did a bad thing in his whole life."

Turning his head toward Jesus, he said, "Please remember me. I believe in you."

"Today you and I will be together with God," said Jesus.

_____ , anyone can decide to believe in Jesus.

Questions
1. Can a person who steals become a friend of Jesus? (Yes)
2. Can we become friends of Jesus? (Yes))
3. Did both thieves decide to be Jesus' friends? (No, only one)

Activity
Make a poster with magazine cutouts of people. Anyone can become a friend of Jesus.

Prayer
Dear Jesus, I pray that all people everywhere might decide to believe in you. Amen.

FRIENDS OF JESUS, FRIENDS OF GOD
Mark 15:33-39; John 19:30

Through Jesus we are now God's friends again. *Romans 5:11*

On the day Jesus died, the whole sky got dark. The darkness lasted from noon (lunch time) until three o'clock (the time in the afternoon when many children come home from school).

Jesus said, "Eloi, Eloi, lama sabachthani." The people thought he called for Elijah to come help him. "Let's see if Elijah comes," they said. They didn't understand.

Then Jesus said, "It is finished." And he died.

_____ , the wrong and sinful things we all do keep us from knowing God. Jesus' death was a punishment for our sin and wrong. When Jesus said, "It is finished," he meant that he had finished the job God asked him to do. Because of Jesus' love for us and what Jesus did, we can be friends of God.

Questions
1. What happened to the sky when Jesus died? (The sky got dark.)
2. Who died to make us friends with God? (Jesus)

Activities
1. Look at a clock or watch. When the short and the long hands are on the 12, it is noon.
2. Tape two craft sticks together to form a cross.

Prayer
Dear Jesus, thank you for dying for me. Thank you for loving me. Thank you for helping me to be friends with God. Amen.

UNCLE MIKE'S VISIT
Romans 5:6-11; Luke 23:44-46

Christ died for us . . . In this way God shows his great love for us.
Romans 5:8

Bobby liked to have his Uncle Mike visit. They read stories together. They played ball together. Sometimes Uncle Mike took Bobby for a ride in his shiny red truck. They had fun.

One nice sunny day, Bobby and Uncle Mike went for a walk behind Bobby's farmhouse. "Look!" said Bobby. "Mr. Barnes has a new little lamb. Let's go see."

"Wait!" yelled Uncle Mike. "There's a car coming!" But Bobby didn't hear. Uncle Mike grabbed Bobby and pushed him back to the side of the road. It was just in time to save Bobby from getting hit by the car. But the car hit Uncle Mike and broke his leg.

Bobby was saved. But Uncle Mike got hit. Uncle Mike loved his nephew and wanted to help him. He didn't want him to get hit by the car. He wanted to save him.

_____ , this is like what Jesus did for us when he died on the cross. We needed someone to help us get to know God. Jesus loved you and me so much that he wanted to help us. He wanted to save us from our sins so we could be friends with God. Jesus wanted to help us to be able to live with God for always.

Questions
1. Who liked to have his Uncle Mike visit? (Bobby)
2. Who loved you and me so much that he died on the cross for us? (Jesus)

Activities
1. Draw a picture of a big truck. Color it red like Uncle Mike's truck.
2. Play catch together.

Prayer
Dear Jesus, thanks for loving and dying for me. You did that so I can know God. And I am very thankful. Amen.

TWO SPECIAL FRIENDS
Matthew 27:57-61; John 19:38-42

Joseph was a secret follower of Jesus. *John 19:38*

Joseph, a leader of the people, believed that Jesus was God's Son, but he was afraid to say so. Maybe he thought the leaders would make fun of him if they knew he believed in Jesus.

But after Jesus died, Joseph decided not to worry about what the others said. He didn't stay quiet about his friendship with Jesus any longer. Joseph and Nicodemus, another friend of Jesus, went to Pilate. "May we take Jesus' body down from the cross?" they asked. "We want to bury him."

"I guess that would be OK," said Pilate.

So Joseph and Nicodemus wrapped Jesus' body in a special cloth. They put his body into a new tomb cut into the side of a big cave. Then they pushed a heavy rock in front of the hole. _____ , Joseph decided to let everyone know that he, too, was a friend of Jesus.

Questions
1. Who was a leader of the people? (Joseph)
2. Did Joseph change his mind about letting people know he was Jesus' friend? (Yes)
3. Who buried Jesus' body? (Joseph and Nicodemus)

Activities
1. Practice saying the names Joseph and Nicodemus.
2. Pretend to roll a heavy rock.

Prayer
Dear Jesus, I'm your friend. I believe you lived and then died for me. I want to let my friends know I love you. Amen.

"MAKES MY FACE HAPPY"
Matthew 28:1-6

Jesus is not here. He has risen from death! *Luke 24:6*

"Tell me again," said Joanie. "I love this part of the story. It makes my face happy."

"OK, honey, here we go," said Mom. "Mary Magdalene and another Mary woke up early. They watched the sun peak over the hills. It was pretty, but it didn't make them feel good. They were sad because their friend Jesus had died. 'Let's go see the place where they buried him,' they said.

"As the two Marys went to the tomb, the ground shook under their feet. 'What's that?' they said. And when they got to the tomb, they found a surprise! The heavy rock that had been in front of the tomb was moved away. An angel had moved it. Now the angel was sitting right on top of the rock. Soldiers guarding the tomb were so frightened that they couldn't talk or move.

"'Don't worry!' the angel told the women. 'I know you're looking for Jesus. But he isn't here. He is alive again, just as he promised. Come and see that the tomb is empty.'"

_____ , this is a happy story. No wonder this story made Joanie smile. Jesus is alive! It's the happy Easter story.

Questions
1. Who sat on top of the heavy rock? (The angel)
2. Who came back alive? (Jesus)

Activity
Make a sad face. Make a surprised face. Make a happy face.

Prayer
Dear Jesus, I like Easter because we celebrate your coming back to life. I know that you are now in Heaven. That makes me want to smile. Amen.

Note to parents/teachers
As a child, I memorized Matthew 28:1-6. Every time I recited it, I wanted to smile. I remember the feeling to this day. "It made my face happy." As a result of experiences like this, I am certain that children are capable of understanding and loving Jesus. May we, as parents and teachers, encourage this childlike faith. — J.C.W.

THE LOCKED DOOR
Luke 24:36-42; John 20:19-29

Those who believe without seeing me will be truly happy.
John 20:29

_____ , do we keep the doors to our house locked at night? Yes, and then we unlock the the door when friends or family want in, don't we?

Jesus' followers had locked their doors after Jesus died. When friends came with the news that Jesus was alive, the followers unlocked a door to let them in. Then they locked the door again.

But while they talked, something happened. Jesus came and stood in the middle of the room. He didn't come through the doors. They were locked. He just came! Jesus' friends were surprised and afraid. Then Jesus said, "It's OK. It's me. Here, touch me!"

Jesus' friend Thomas wasn't in the room that day. When the others told Thomas what happened, he said, "Until I see the nail marks in Jesus' hands, I won't believe he is alive."

The next week Jesus came again. This time Thomas was there. Jesus said, "It's me! See my hands!" Thomas looked at the hurt marks in Jesus' hands. He said, "It is you, Jesus."

"You believe because you've seen me," Jesus said. "Other people will decide to believe without seeing me."

Jesus was talking about you and me when he said those words. We can decide to believe that Jesus is alive and wants to be our friend.

Questions
1. Did Jesus come through the door of the room? (No)
2. Who said he wouldn't believe until he saw Jesus' hands? (Thomas)

Activity
Show your child your keys. Show him how the door to your house locks and unlocks.

Prayer
Jesus, I believe you're alive even though I can't see you in this room with me right now. It makes me happy to believe and love you. Amen.

A FISH STORY
John 21:1-14

It is the Lord! *John 21:7*

_____ , do you know anyone who likes to fish? Jesus' friends liked to fish, too. And when they felt lonely without Jesus, they decided to go fishing. They fished all night.

The next morning a man stood on the beach. "Caught any fish yet?" he shouted.

"No, we fished all night, but we don't have even one fish," they answered.

"Put your fishing net into the water on the other side of the boat," said the man. So Jesus' friends tried this. Boy, were they surprised! They caught so many fish they couldn't lift the heavy net back into the boat.

John looked at all the fish. Then he looked at the man on the beach. "That must be Jesus!" he said.

Jesus' friends pulled the heavy net full of fish to the shore. The man on the beach was Jesus! He said, "Come on over to the fire. I'm making breakfast." Then they all knew that Jesus was alive again. No one else could do the special things that Jesus did.

Questions
1. Who liked to fish? (Jesus' friends)
2. Who was the man on the beach? (Jesus)
3. Did Jesus help his friends catch fish? (Yes)

Activities
1. Count as high as you can. (There were 153 fish.)
2. Pretend to go fishing. The floor is the water. Your bed or chair is the boat.

Prayer
Dear Jesus, thank you for showing your friends that you were alive. We believe that today you are alive in Heaven with God. Amen.

"GOOD-BYE FOR NOW"
Matthew 28:16-20; Luke 24:50-53

Go everywhere in the world. Tell the Good News to everyone.
Mark 16:15

_____ , who came back to life at Easter time? Yes, Jesus did. Jesus' helper-friends were so glad Jesus was alive again. But now it was time for Jesus to go back and live with his Father God in Heaven. He and his friends had to say good-bye.

"Meet me on the hill in Galilee," said Jesus. "I'll be waiting for you there."

His friends climbed the hill together. When they reached the top, they saw Jesus. They knew their friend Jesus was different from anyone else. He never did anything wrong. He loved people like no one else ever had. He had died and was alive again.

Jesus said, "My friends, go and tell other people about me. Tell the people where you live. Tell the people across the water. Tell all people everywhere. Anyone can become my friend. All people are invited to join me in Heaven.

"Teach people to obey everything I've taught you. I will be with you always. And I am sending you a helper to be with you. He will help you when you're scared or lonely or tired. Good-bye for now." Then Jesus went to Heaven.

Questions
1. Who said, "Go and tell other people about me?" (Jesus)
2. Who is invited to be Jesus' friend? (All people)

Activity
Take a walk. Do you have a hill nearby? Perhaps you can walk up the hill together.

Prayer
Dear Jesus, I know you're in Heaven now with God. Thank you for loving all the people in the whole world. I pray that people everywhere will want to become your friend. Amen.

BOOKS, BOOKS, AND MORE BOOKS
John 20:30, 31; 21:25

Jesus did many other miracles . . . that are not written in this book.
John 20:30

_____ , do you like to read? Would you like to write a book someday? A long time ago there was a little girl who wanted to write a book about Jesus. "I'll write about the people Jesus loved and helped," she said. "I'll write down the things he said about his Father God."

When the girl grew up and went away to college, she kept writing about all the good things Jesus did. She married and had a little girl. She told her daughter about her friend Jesus. All her life she wrote stories about Jesus. One day she said, "It's time for me to go live with Jesus in Heaven." Still she had not finished writing about all the special things Jesus did.

This story of the little girl writer is make-believe. But it helps us understand how John felt when he wrote the book of John in the Bible. He said, "There are many other great things that Jesus did. If every one of them were written down, I think the whole world would not be big enough for all books that would be written" (John 21:25).

There is no one like our friend Jesus. He is wonderful.

Questions
1. Whom did the little girl want to write about? (Jesus)
2. Who wrote the book of John? (John)

Activities
1. Open the Bible to the book of John.
2. Put your hands together to form a book and pretend to read a story about Jesus.

Prayer
Jesus, there is no one like you. You are the best friend and helper I've ever had. Amen.

DECISIONS! DECISIONS!
Acts 1:12-26

Lord, . . . show us which one . . . you have chosen to do this work.
Acts 1:24

Judas had been one of Jesus' special helpers, but then he decided to help the people who arrested Jesus. After Jesus rose again and went back to Heaven, Peter said, "Since Judas isn't one of us anymore, we must find another man to do his job. Let's choose a man who knows and loves Jesus."

"Lord God, help us now," prayed Jesus' friends. "Only you know what each man is thinking. Show us which man you want to take Judas' place and be your apostle."

Jesus was back to Heaven, so he wasn't at the meeting to help them decide. And God had not yet sent the Holy Spirit to help them decide. So they prayed to God and then threw "lots" to choose. Lots were little stones. The apostles threw them on the ground. The way they landed helped the apostles decide.

In Bible times, this was a common way for people to make decisions. Many times God controlled the way the lots fell to let people know what he wanted them to do. But today, Christians have God's Holy Spirit living within them to help them make good decisions.

Matthias was the man chosen to take Judas' place. _____, God answered the apostles' prayer and helped them with the decision.

Questions
1. Which apostle decided not to be Jesus' friend? (Judas)
2. Who was the new apostle? (Matthias)

Activity
Name times that a young child might need to make a decision.

Prayer
Dear God, the apostles asked you to help them make the right decision. Help me, too, when I have to decide. Amen.

NOISY LIKE THE WIND
Acts 2:1-12

They were all filled with the Holy Spirit. Acts 2:4

_____ , you know what it sounds like when a strong wind blows against your window, don't you? Can you show me what it sounds like?

Jesus' friends heard a noise even louder than that. When the sound of a strong wind filled the house where they were, something special happened to Jesus' friends. They felt it. They heard it. They knew it. Jesus said it would happen. And it did. The Holy Spirit came to live inside each one of them. They all started to talk in other languages.

Many people from other countries were visiting in the city that day. They were surprised when Jesus' friends began to talk with words they understood. God's Holy Spirit was helping Jesus' friends talk so that the visitors could understand.

Jesus wasn't right there with them anymore, so God sent his Holy Spirit to help them tell others about Jesus. This same Holy Spirit helps us today. He helps us learn to love, pray, and not be afraid.

Questions
1. What does wind sound like?
2. Who talked in other languages? (Jesus' friends)
3. Who helps us learn to love, pray, and not be afraid? (The Holy Spirit)

Activities
1. Make a blowing sound through an empty paper tube.
2. Learn some words from a foreign language.

Prayer
Dear God, thank you for the Holy Spirit. He is my friend. Amen.

THE NIGHTTIME SURPRISE
Acts 5:12-21

Don't be upset when others get rich or when someone else's plans succeed. Psalm 37:7

_____ , after the church began, God did wonderful things every day.

Jesus' friends taught about God. Men, women, and children who were sick got well again. People started to love and believe in Jesus.

But the leaders of the people weren't happy. They wanted the people to listen only to them. The leaders were jealous. They grabbed Jesus' friends and put them in jail.

During the night, God surprised everyone. An angel opened up the doors of the jail. "Now go to the temple and teach again," said the angel. "Tell the people how much Jesus loves them and how he will help them have a good life."

So Jesus' friends did just what the angel said.

Questions
1. What wonderful things did God do? (Jesus' friends taught about God; sick people got well; people started to believe in Jesus.)
2. Who wasn't happy about these great things? (The leaders)
3. Who went to jail? (Jesus' friends)
4. Who opened the jail door? (God's angel)

Activities
1. Name some good things that have happened to a friend. (Ideas: a new toy, a trip, a visit from grandparents, an award)
2. Choose a way to tell a friend you are happy for him.

Prayer
Dear God, help me to be glad when good things happen to other people. Amen.

GAMALIEL'S IDEA
Acts 5:17-42

But if it is from God, you will not be able to stop them. *Acts 5:39*

_____ , how did Jesus' friends get out of jail? Yes, God's angel surprised them during the night, opened the door, and let them out.

When the temple leaders learned that Jesus' friends were out of jail and teaching about Jesus again, they were angry. "You're making trouble for us again!" they yelled. "We told you not to teach about Jesus. And you are doing it anyway!"

Peter said, "We must obey God, not men. You killed Jesus. But the same God you worship made Jesus come back alive. God wants you to know this."

These words made the leaders so angry that they wanted to kill Jesus' friends right then. But a man named Gamaliel said, "Be careful what you do to these men. If what they do and say is just their own idea, it won't last. People will forget about them. But if what they are teaching is from God, we won't be able to stop them."

The leaders listened to Gamaliel. They let Jesus' friends go. And Jesus' friends were happy to be teaching the good news about Jesus and his love.

Questions
1. Who was angry? (The temple leaders)
2. Who said, "Be careful, because these men's words may be from from God"? (Gamaliel)

Activity
Write the letters G-a-m-a-l-i-e-l on a piece of paper. Have your child copy the letters. Name each letter together.

Prayer
Dear God, I want to obey you and not people who might tell me to forget about Jesus. Amen.

STEPHEN'S STORY
Acts 6:8 — 7:60

I see the Son of Man standing at God's right side! *Acts 7:56*

_____ , Stephen loved God. The Holy Spirit helped Stephen do wonderful things. But some people didn't like him because they didn't want to hear about Jesus. These people tried to argue with Stephen, but God gave Stephen the right words to say. Then the people couldn't think of anything bad to say back to him. So they lied about him, and they gave money to others to say more lies about Stephen.

The people's leaders were angry. Everyone watched Stephen to see what he would do. They saw that Stephen's face was not angry or afraid. Stephen knew God was helping him.

Stephen told the people true stories about God and about their heroes, like Abraham and Moses. "God keeps his promises," Stephen said. "You need to believe that Jesus is God's Son."

But the leaders did not want to hear about Jesus. They took Stephen outside and threw rocks at him to hurt him. But God let Stephen see into Heaven. "I see Jesus in Heaven with God!" Stephen cried. "I'm going to go there now." Then Stephen died.

Questions
1. Who loved God? (Stephen)
2. Why did some people want to hurt Stephen? (They didn't want to hear about Jesus.)
3. Where did Stephen go? (To Heaven to be with God and Jesus)

Activity
Take a walk and look at rocks. Talk about how important it is not to throw rocks at anyone or anything.

Prayer
Dear Jesus, Stephen loved, believed, and talked to you. Even when people lied about him, he prayed and told the truth. Help me to tell the truth about myself and you. Amen.

SCATTERED
Acts 8:1-4

*And everywhere they were scattered, they told people
the Good News. Acts 8:4*

People who believe that Jesus is God's Son are called "the
church." On the same day Stephen died, some of the people and
leaders began to do things to hurt the church in the city of
Jerusalem.

One man named Saul worked hard to get rid of people who
believed in Jesus. He went to every house and knocked on the
door. "Do you believe in Jesus?" he asked. If they said yes, he beat
them and put them in jail.

So Jesus' friends moved to other cities in Judea and Samaria to
get away from Saul. Wherever they moved, they kept telling people about Jesus. The good news about Jesus spread to more cities.
Every day more people learned about Jesus.

The "good news" is also called the "gospel." It is the true story
that Jesus lived, died for us, and rose from the dead to live again. If
we believe this, we can know God and live with him forever. This
is good news!

Questions

1. Who are the people who are
   called the church? (People who
   believe in Jesus)
2. Who threw Jesus' followers in
   jail? (Saul)
3. Where did Jesus' friends go to get
   away from Saul? (They moved
   away to other cities in Judea and
   Samaria.)

Activities
1. Talk about what it is like to move to another place.
2. Show your child a map of Jerusalem, Judea, and Samaria. (Look
   in the back of your Bible.)

Prayer
Dear God, Jesus' friends told about Jesus wherever they went.
Help me to tell about Jesus to anyone who wants to hear. Amen.

MOVING TO A NEW PLACE
Acts 8:5-8

Many of the Samaritans . . . believed in Jesus. *John 4:39*

_____ , where do we live? *(Pause for an answer.)* Most of Jesus' followers lived in the city of Jerusalem. But when the leaders started to put Jesus' friends in jail, some moved to Samaria. Do you remember when Jesus stopped to rest in Samaria? He asked a woman there for a drink. After Jesus talked to her, the woman believed in him. She told all her friends about Jesus. Now Jesus' followers were moving to this place called Samaria.

Philip was one of those who went to Samaria. The Samaritan people liked Philip, and they listened to him talk about Jesus. Many believed the true stories Philip told about Jesus. God helped Philip do special and wonderful things. The people in the city of Samaria were very happy to hear about Jesus.

Questions
1. Where did some of Jesus' friends go to live? (Samaria)
2. Who taught about Jesus in Samaria? (Philip)
3. Were the Samaritans happy to hear about Jesus? (Yes)

Activities
1. What are the people in your city called?
2. Draw a picture with crowds of smiling people.

Prayer
Dear Jesus, you love all people, no matter where they live, in Jerusalem or Samaria, in the United States or far away. All people can know you, love you, and be your friend. That makes me smile. Amen.

THE MAGIC MAN
Acts 8:9-25

You thought you could buy God's gift with money. *Acts 8:20*

Simon lived in Samaria. People liked to watch him do magic tricks. "I'm a great man," Simon bragged. "Look at everything I can do." Some people thought Simon's magic was from God. They were wrong.

Philip moved to the city of Samaria and taught about Jesus. Simon decided to believe in Jesus. Simon saw Philip do great things, and he was amazed.

Then the apostles came to Samaria. They prayed for the believers to receive the Holy Spirit. Simon wanted to do the same miracles that the apostles did. "Here's some money," said Simon. "Now help me do these things, too. "

Peter heard Simon. "You don't understand, Simon," said Peter. "You can't buy God's help. Change your thinking. Tell God you're sorry for thinking you could buy his help."

_____ , you and I cannot buy God's love. We can't even try to get God to love us. He loves us just as we are. He wants us to believe in Jesus. God gives us his love as a gift. We cannot buy it with money.

Questions
1. Who did magic tricks? (Simon)
2. Who taught about Jesus in Samaria? (Philip)
3. What did Simon try to buy? (God's help, so he could do miracles)

Activity
Look at some pennies, dimes, and quarters. Count them. Talk about what you could buy with the money. Talk about what you could not buy.

Prayer
Dear God, I know I cannot buy your love or the Holy Spirit's help. But I know I need you. Thank you for your gift of love to me. Amen.

THE CHARIOT MAN
Acts 8:26-40

Make followers of all people in the world. *Matthew 28:19*

One day an angel came to Philip. "Start traveling south," said the angel. "Go down the desert road." Philip didn't know why he should go down that road. But he did.

On Philip's walk down that road, he saw a man riding in a chariot. "Go closer," said God's Spirit. When Philip got close, he could hear the man reading from a book of the Old Testament.

"Do you know what you're reading?" asked Philip.

"No," said the man. "I need someone to help me understand."

"I'll help," said Philip. "You're reading about Jesus. He's God's Son and my friend."

_____ , that day the man in the chariot decided to make Jesus his friend, too.

The man in the chariot came from Ethiopia, in Africa. God wanted the good news about Jesus to be heard by people in other countries, too. The man went back to his country full of joy.

Questions
1. Who saw a man sitting in a chariot? (Philip)
2. What was the man in the chariot reading? (A book from the Old Testament)
3. Who decided to be Jesus' friend? (The man in the chariot)

Activities
1. Look at a map together. Show your child north, south, east, and west.
2. The road to your house goes _____ .

Prayer
Dear God, I like being Jesus' friend. I pray that _____ might decide to be Jesus' friend, too. Amen. *(Insert a friend or relative's name in the blank space.)*

THE FLASHING LIGHT
Acts 9:1-6

If anyone belongs to Christ, then he is made new.
2 Corinthians 5:17

Saul hated every man and woman, boy and girl who loved and followed Jesus. He spent his days looking for the friends of Jesus. "If you don't stop this Jesus stuff, I'm going to get you," said Saul. Most of the time, he threw Jesus' friends in jail.

One day something happened that changed everything. As Saul traveled on the road to Damascus, a bright light flashed all around him. Saul fell down. Then he heard a voice. "Saul, why do you keep doing these things to hurt me?"

"Who's talking?" asked Saul.

"I'm Jesus. When you hurt my friends, you hurt me, too," answered the voice. "Get up and go on into the city. Wait there. Soon someone will tell you what to do next."

Saul stood up. "I can't see," he said. The men with him took his hand and led him into the city of Damascus to wait.

_____ , God sent the bright light to get Saul to listen to him. He wanted to change Saul's heart of hate to a heart of love. God planned to change Saul's whole life.

Questions
1. Where was Saul going? (Damascus)
2. What happened to Saul on the road? (A light flashed, he fell, and a voice spoke.)
3. Who said, "You hurt me when you hurt my friends?" (Jesus)

Activity
Close your eyes tightly. Discuss how it feels to be without sight.

Prayer
Dear God, you helped Saul want to change. I know you can help me, too. Amen.

PRAYING AND FORGETTING TO WORRY
Acts 9:7-16

Do not worry . . . But pray. *Philippians 4:6*

Close your eyes, _____ . You can't see me sitting here, can you? It's a funny feeling to see only darkness, isn't it? Maybe Saul had that funny feeling, too. After the flashing light came on Saul, he fell down. His friends led him into town. For three days he couldn't see, he didn't eat, and he didn't drink. He just waited. While he waited, he prayed. In a vision — something like a dream — from the Lord, Saul saw a man named Ananias come to help him.

At the same time, the Lord spoke to the man named Ananias.. "Get up and go to Straight Street," he said. "Find Saul. He'll be ready to see you."

"I've heard about Saul," said Ananias. "He hurts everyone who loves Jesus. That means he might get me, too."

"It's OK, Ananias," the Lord said. "Saul is changing. I have a special job for him to do."

So Ananias believed God and forgot about his worrying. When we pray and really believe God will help us, we can forget about our worrying, too.

Questions
1. Who waited for Ananias to come? (Saul)
2. Who believed God and forgot about worrying? (Ananias)

Activity
Take a walk with your eyes closed. Have someone you trust lead you by the hand.

Prayer
Dear God, I know you care about my family and me, just as you cared about Saul and Ananias. Help us to forget about worrying and believe you will help us with everything we do. Amen.

CHANGED!
Acts 9:10-22

In Christ Jesus, God made us new people so that we would do good works. *Ephesians 2:10*

"Saul, the Lord Jesus sent me to see you," said Ananias. "He is the one you saw on the road. He sent me to help you see again and to be filled with the Holy Spirit."

Right away something fell off Saul's eyes. "I can see!" he said. Then Saul got up, ate, and felt much better. Saul stayed with the friends of Jesus for a few more days. Then he started teaching the good news about Jesus.

"Isn't this amazing?" said the people. "This is the same man who came here to throw us in jail. He's really changed."

_____ , Saul decided to believe God's words about Jesus. He made up his mind to follow Jesus. We can make up our minds, too. When Ananias did what the Lord asked *him* to do, Saul got his sight back and began to tell others about Jesus.

Questions
1. Who came to see Saul? (Ananias)
2. Who sent Ananias to Saul? (Jesus)
3. What did Saul begin to do? (Teach about Jesus)

Activity
Draw a picture of Ananias and Saul.

Prayer
Dear Jesus, you changed Saul's ideas. He decided to be your friend. I want to be your friend, too. Teach me more about what it means to know you. Amen.

LOOK! HE'S OUT OF BED!
Acts 9:32-35

Jesus Christ heals you. *Acts 9:34*

Peter traveled from town to town, visiting the people who believed in Jesus. In one town he met a man named Aeneas, who had been in bed for eight years. _____ , that's a long time to stay in bed, isn't it?

"Aeneas, Jesus makes you well," said Peter. "Stand up now and make your bed."

Aeneas didn't wait. Right away he stood up. And he made his bed!

The people in the town and all around knew that only God could make Aeneas well. After this, many people decided to believed in Jesus.

Questions
1. Who went from town to town talking about his friend, Jesus? (Peter)
2. How long was the man in bed? (Eight years)
3. Who made the man well? (Peter said, "Jesus makes you well.")
4. Who believed in Jesus? (People of the town and all around)

Activities
1. Count to eight.
2. Make a bed.

Prayer
Dear Jesus, I know that you're the one who made the man well. I know that you're the one who makes people better today, too. Please help my sick friend _____ . Thank you. Amen. *(Fill in the blank with the name of someone you and your child know.)*

GOD LOVES US ALL
Acts 10:34-43

To God every person is the same. *Acts 10:34*

_____ , some people are big. Other people are little. Some have dark skin and some have light skin. Some children are born in the United States and some are born in other countries. It doesn't matter to God. He loves us all. God wants children, moms, and dads everywhere to know and love him.

Cornelius loved God, but he had not heard the good news about Jesus. Many people thought that only Jews could believe in Jesus. Then God told Peter that anyone could believe in Jesus.

"Every person is the same to me," said God. "I say the same words to all people. It doesn't matter where a child is born. Any person can believe and love my Son Jesus."

So Peter told Cornelius and his friends. And while he was talking, the Holy Spirit came. Everyone was happy. This was very good news!

God loves us all! It is good news for you and me, too.

Questions

1. Does it matter to God where a child is born? (No)
2. Whom does God love? (He loves everyone of us.)
3. Who can believe in Jesus? (Anyone who wants to)

Activities

1. Name different kinds of people whom God loves. (Ideas: big and little, light and dark, rich and poor, blind and sighted)
2. Draw a picture of a short man and a tall man.

Prayer

Dear God, I'm glad that every person is the same to you. I am little, but you love me. My daddy (or grandpa or uncle) is big, and you love him, too. Thank you for loving us all. Amen.

COULD I STOP GOD?
Acts 11:1-18

The Good News . . . is the power God uses to save everyone who believes — to save the Jews first, and also to save the non-Jews. Romans 1:16

Peter stayed with Cornelius and his friends for a few days. He liked visiting them. But when Peter got back home, his Jewish friends said, "Peter, how could you eat with those people! They're different! You know God loves us more than he loves them!"

Then Peter told them everything. He told them about his special dream. He told them that God said, "Every person is the same to me!" He told them about going to see Cornelius and his friends.

"God gave the Holy Spirit to them, too. Could I stop God from doing that?" asked Peter. "No way!"

So Peter's Jewish friends changed their minds. "Thank you, God," they said. "You are good and kind to all people. Any man, woman, or child can choose to love you."

Questions
1. Did Peter's friends like it that he ate with Cornelius? (No)
2. Did they change their minds? (Yes)

Activity
Sing "Jesus Loves the Little Children."

Prayer
Dear God, thank you that you love all the children of the world. Amen.

PRAYING FRIENDS
Acts 12:1-5

But the church kept on praying to God for him. *Acts 12:5*

Everywhere Peter went, he did good things. He helped people. He talked to them about his friend, Jesus. Many people liked Peter.

But mean King Herod Agrippa didn't like Peter. He didn't like Jesus, either. He didn't like people doing good things. So the king grabbed Peter and put him in jail. "Ha! Ha! Now Peter can't do all those good things," said King Herod. "Being in jail will shut him up."

The king ordered sixteen big soldiers to guard Peter. Herod wanted to make sure Peter didn't get away.

While Peter was in jail, his friends prayed to God. "Please keep Peter from getting hurt," they asked. "And help him get out of jail."

_____ , you and I can pray for our friends when they need God's help, too.

Questions
1. Who talked about his friend Jesus? (Peter)
2. What was the mean king's name? (King Herod Agrippa)
3. Where did King Herod Agrippa put Peter? (In jail)
4. How many soldiers stood guard around Peter? (sixteen)
5. Who prayed for Peter while he was in jail? (His friends)

Activities
1. Count to sixteen.
2. Name friends that you can pray for today.

Prayer
Dear God, Peter's friends prayed for him. I want to pray for my friends, too. Please help _____ and _____ . Thanks. Amen.

WHEN IT'S DARK
Acts 12:6-12

When you lie down, your sleep will be peaceful.
Proverbs 3:24

The jail was an icky, dirty place. Peter was handcuffed with heavy chains to a big soldier on his left side and a big soldier on his right side. Other soldiers were outside the door.

But do you know what, _____? Peter wasn't worried. "God will take care of me," he thought. "I guess I'll close my eyes and go to sleep." And he did.

In the night, Peter felt something. An angel had touched his side to wake him up. "Hurry! Get up, Peter!" said the angel. "Get dressed." Right away Peter's chains came off. "Follow me," said the angel.

Peter and the angel walked past the soldiers, out the front door, and down the street. Then poof! The angel disappeared. "God really took care of me!" said Peter.

Questions
1. Was the jail a nice place? (No)
2. Who didn't worry, closed his eyes, and went to sleep? (Peter)
3. Who woke up Peter? (An angel)
4. Did God take care of Peter? (Yes)

Activities
1. Tie your child's hand and your hand together with a ribbon. Pretend you are handcuffed together.
2. Draw a picture of Peter and the angel.

Prayer
Dear God, you helped Peter stop worrying and go to sleep. Please help me to go to sleep in my own bed without worrying. Thanks. Amen.

MISSIONARY FRIENDS
Acts 13:1-3

How beautiful is the person who comes over the mountains
to bring good news. *Isaiah 52:7*

_____ , do you remember learning about Saul? Saul's name was changed to Paul after he believed in Jesus.

Some other people had a new name, too. In the town of Antioch, all the people who believed in Jesus were called "Christians." That means "belonging to Christ." Soon all believers everywhere were called Christians.

One day God's Holy Spirit said to the Christians in Antioch, "Paul and Barnabas are going to do a special job for me. Please help them get ready."

So the Christians prayed together for Paul and Barnabas. And then Paul and Barnabas left the city to go on a long trip. They were going to be missionaries for God. A missionary is a person who goes (sometimes to a faraway place) to tell and teach about Jesus. Missionaries are Jesus' friends. Do you know any missionaries?

Questions
1. What does the word "Christian" mean? (Belonging to Christ)
2. Who prayed for Paul and Barnabas? (The Christians in Antioch)
3. What is a missionary? (A person who goes — sometimes to a faraway place — to tell and teach others about Jesus.)

Activities
1. Name any missionaries you know.
2. Write their names in the blanks of the prayer below.

Prayer
Dear God, please help _____ and _____ when they teach or talk about Jesus. Help those who are listening to them to understand and believe in Jesus, too. Amen.

TELLING THE TRUTH
Acts 13:4-12

Truth will last forever. But lies last only a moment.
Proverbs 12:19

Paul and Barnabas sailed in a boat to an island. _____ , do you know what an island is? An island is land that has water all around it.

On the island was a man named Elymas who did magic and pretended to love God. Elymas was a troublemaker. He didn't like Paul and Barnabas, and he didn't want anyone on the island to believe in Jesus.

One day, God's Holy Spirit told Paul to say, "Elymas, you're always telling lies and trying to fool people by doing bad tricks. You tell people that God's words are lies. Well, God wants you to stop doing that. You're going to be blind for a little while."

Then everything went dark for Elymas. He walked around trying to find someone to take his hand and lead him around. When the leader of the island saw what had happened, he decided to believe in Jesus.

Questions
1. What is an island? (Land with water all around it)
2. Whom did Paul and Barnabas meet on the island? (Elymas)
3. What happened to Elymas? (He could not see.)

Activity
Sit in a chair and pretend to be on the island with Paul and Barnabas.

Prayer
Dear God, I know that you don't like lying. Please help me always to tell the truth. Amen.

GOOD NEWS
Acts 13:13-43

We tell you the Good News. *Acts 13:32*

_____ , missionary friends Paul and Barnabas moved from town to town. One day they walked into a synagogue and sat down to listen. When the synagogue leaders saw Paul and Barnabas, they said, "Men, if you have any good words for us, please stand up and tell us."

So Paul stood up. "All you who love and pray to God, please listen," he said. "I want to tell you something very important. Long ago God chose the Israelites to be his special people. He helped them leave Egypt, where they were slaves. He gave them lots of babies and helped them grow. He gave them a new land with new homes. He took care of them for 450 years.

"Then he gave them two strong kings named Saul and David. And God promised that one day he would send a special one to earth. Jesus is that special one. He came to earth and was killed, but God made him alive again. Now Jesus lives with God in Heaven.

"This is a true story. When you believe in Jesus, God forgives and forgets about the wrong things you do and say. This is Good News."

When Paul and Barnabas left the synagogue, the leaders asked them to come back and teach the next week.

Questions
1. Who moved from city to city? (Paul and Barnabas)
2. Where did Paul teach? (Synagogue)

Activity
Pretend to be a teacher like Paul. Tell your "class" something about Jesus.

Prayer
Dear God, thank you for Jesus. I believe in him. Amen.

Note to parents/teachers
The word *synagogue* means "a meeting." It is the place where the Jewish people met to read and study the Scripture. The Jewish people were once called Israelites.

CUDDLING WITH GRANDMA
Acts 13:44-46

Where there is jealousy and selfishness, there will be confusion.
James 3:16

_____ , it's fun to spend time with Grandma, isn't it? Tony liked being with his grandma, too. "Grandma, read me a story, please," said Tony.

"OK, Tony, but you'll have to wait," answered Grandma. "I'm combing Tammy's hair now. When I'm through, I'll read a story to both of you."

Tony frowned. Then he had an idea. "Grandma, it's time for Tammy's nap now," he said. "Mom doesn't read her stories, anyway. She's kind of little, you know!"

"Why, Tony, you know your sister just woke up," said Grandma. Tony made a grouchy face.

"What's wrong, Tony?" asked Grandma.

"I want you to read just to me," said Tony, "and not to Tammy, too. I said it was time for Tammy's nap so you could read just to me."

"Tony, I love you and Tammy, too!" said Grandma. "Come here so I can hold you both."

Tony walked over to the rocking chair. He climbed on Grandma's lap. So did Tammy. They cuddled close. "Let's read a story together," said Grandma.

Questions
1. Who wanted Grandma to read him a story? (Tony)
2. Whom did Grandma love? (Tony and Tammy)
3. Did Tony let Grandma read to both Tammy and him? (Yes)

Activities
1. Sit in the rocking chair and cuddle.
2. Make a frowning face. Make a grouchy face. Make a loving, happy face.
3. Draw a picture of yourself with a happy face and send it to a grandparent.

Prayer
Dear God, help me to share and not be jealous. Please help me tell the truth. Thanks. Amen.

MEAN WORDS
Acts 13:44-46

I trust in God. I will not be afraid. What can people do to me?
Psalm 56:11

_____ , have you ever been at a place where there were lots and lots of people?

When Paul and Barnabas talked about Jesus at the synagogue, many people came. The leaders weren't happy about the crowd. They were jealous. They wanted the people to like them best. They didn't want the people to listen to Paul and Barnabas, and they said mean words to Paul and Barnabas.

But Paul and Barnabas weren't afraid. "We're going to do and say what God wants even if you don't like it," they said.

Someday, someone might say mean words to us when we talk about Jesus. We don't have to be afraid. It is better to do what God wants us to do than to be afraid of other people.

Questions
1. Were there lots of people waiting to hear Paul and Barnabas talk about Jesus? (Yes)
2. Who wasn't happy about this? (The jealous leaders)
3. What is it called when you want someone to like you best? (Being jealous)
4. Were Paul and Barnabas afraid? (No)

Activity
Draw a picture of Paul and Barnabas talking about Jesus.

Prayer
Dear God, you are with me all the time, even when people say mean things. Help me not to be afraid. Thank you. Amen.

DECIDING ABOUT JESUS
Acts 13:46-52

You must choose for yourselves today. You must decide
whom you will serve. *Joshua 24:15*

"We've always told you the truth about Jesus," said Paul and
Barnabas to the leaders of the Jewish people. "We wanted to tell
you this good news before we told other people. But you've decided not to believe and follow
Jesus. So now we're going to go
tell other people about Jesus."

This made the non-Jewish
people very happy. They wanted
to hear about Jesus. Right away
many of them decided to follow
Jesus.

But the jealous leaders still
were unhappy. They made trouble for Paul and Barnabas. So
Paul and Barnabas left and went
to a different city.

When we make a decision, we "choose." We make up our
mind to do, say, or believe something. Each day we choose, or
decide, what to wear. We choose, or decide, to do what Mom (or
Dad) says. We choose, or decide, to eat an apple or an orange. But
our most important choice is deciding to believe and love God.

_____ , we can't make anyone else believe and follow
Jesus. Each person — boy, girl, or grown-up — needs to decide for
himself.

Questions
1. Who told the truth about Jesus? (Paul and Barnabas)
2. Can we make someone else believe Jesus? (No)

Activity
Make a decision about which clothes to wear, which toy to play
with, or what to eat for a snack.

Prayer
Dear God, I know I can't make my friends believe in you. But
please help my friends want to decide to follow Jesus. Amen.

HE'S WALKING!
Acts 14:8-17

And in all you do, give thanks to God the Father through Jesus.
Colossians 3:17

_____ , have you ever seen a person who couldn't walk? One day Paul and Barnabas met a man whose legs didn't work. He couldn't walk. The man listened quietly while Paul talked about God. Then Paul saw that the man believed God could heal him. "Stand up on your feet!" said Paul. And the man did something he had never done before. He stood. He jumped. He walked around. He ran.

All the people heard Paul say, "Stand up!" They saw the man jump up. They thought Paul and Barnabas had made the man walk. They didn't understand who really made the man's legs work.

Paul and Barnabas were sorry that the people were mixed up about what happened. "God made the man walk," said Paul. "The same God who made the sky, the earth, and all the animals and people. He's the healer. We're men just like you. We're here to tell you about God's Son and our friend, Jesus."

Questions
1. Who met a man who couldn't walk? (Paul and Barnabas)
2. What did Paul say to him? ("Stand up!")
3. Who made the man walk? (God)

Activities
1. Talk about what it might be like to be unable to walk.
2. Draw a picture of the man before he could walk and after he could walk.

Prayer
Dear God, you made everything. You are the God who helps people get well. I know that people can't do the things that you can do. You are great. Amen.

THE EARTHQUAKE
Acts 16:22-32

*About midnight Paul and Silas were praying
and singing songs to God. Acts 16:25*

_____ , do you know what an earthquake is? An earthquake is when the ground shakes under your feet. Sometimes pictures fall off the wall. Huge cracks can come in the road. Sometimes houses fall down. Listen to a story about an earthquake that happened long ago.

"You're troublemakers!" shouted the people. They hit Paul and his helper, Silas. Then they threw them in jail. The jailer was afraid they would try to get away, so he put them in a room far away from the door. He chained their feet to a wooden post. They couldn't move. Their hands hurt. Their feet hurt. It was hard to sleep.

But Paul and Silas didn't cry or yell. Do you know what they did? They prayed, and they sang songs to God. The other prisoners listened to their songs in the middle of the night.

Suddenly, there was a loud rumble. Everyone's chains dropped off. The jail doors swung open. And the jailer shook with fear. He was afraid he would be killed if the prisoners were gone.

"It's OK!" shouted Paul. "We're all still here."

So the jailer ran inside and fell down in front of Paul. "How can I be saved?" he asked.

"Believe in Jesus," said Paul and Silas. Then the happy jailer believed, and his life changed.

Questions
1. Who was thrown in jail? (Paul and Silas)
2. What happened in the jail? (An earthquake)

Activity
Sing a happy song to God.

Prayer
Dear Jesus, help me to sing and pray to you even when things don't go right. Amen.

TEACHERS ARE OUR FRIENDS
Acts 18:18-28

Respect those people who work hard with you, who lead you in the Lord and teach you. 1 Thessalonians 5:12

Teachers can be Jesus' friends, too. Paul had two teacher friends named Priscilla and Aquila. Sometimes this married couple traveled with Paul. Others times they stayed home. One day Priscilla and Aquila met another teacher named Apollos. Apollos knew a lot about the Scriptures. But Apollos didn't know about the wonderful things that had happened to Peter and Paul and all Jesus' friends since Jesus had gone back to Heaven.

"Let's take Apollos home with us," said Priscilla and her husband, Aquila. "We can teach him what we've learned."

Apollos listened and learned. Teachers Priscilla and Aquila helped Apollos. When Apollos left, he wanted to teach about Jesus wherever he could.

_____ , teachers help us learn. We can pray for our teachers. Teachers can be Jesus' friends, too.

Questions
1. Who sometimes traveled with Paul? (Priscilla and Aquila)
2. Where did Priscilla and Aquila take Apollos? (To their home)
3. Who help us learn? (Teachers)
4. Can teachers be Jesus' friends, too? (Yes)

Activities
1. Play school together, with your child as the teacher.
2. Name a Sunday school or preschool teacher. Write a thank-you note to that teacher, if appropriate. Thank him or her for teaching you so many good things.

Prayer
Dear God, thank you for teachers. Help them to have patience and energy. And help them to have good ideas for teaching. Amen.

MAYBE YES — MAYBE NO
Acts 26:1-32

"Do you think you can persuade me to become a Christian in such a short time?" Acts 26:28

Paul had done nothing wrong. Still he was thrown in jail because he talked about Jesus.

A king named Agrippa listened to Paul's story. "I used to hurt Jesus' friends," said Paul. "But I changed my mind. I now believe Jesus is the one God promised to send. You know about that, too, Agrippa. You studied about that just like me."

"Paul, if I listened to you anymore, I just might decide to believe," said King Agrippa. "But I guess I won't right now."

"I pray that all people who hear about Jesus will decide to become his friend," said Paul.

_____ , anyone can be Jesus' friend. But not everyone decides to believe the truth about Jesus. Some people say "Yes." Some people say "No." And some say, "Maybe later."

God loves us so much that he lets us make up our own minds about whether we want to be Jesus' friends. What is your decision?

Questions
1. Was it fair that Paul was in jail? (No)
2. Did King Agrippa decide to become Jesus' friend? (No, not then)

Activity
Pretend to be a king. Dress up in a robe. Make a crown out of construction paper or foil.

Prayer
Dear God, thank you for giving us the choice to be Jesus' friends. Amen.

SAILING TO ROME
Acts 28:1-30; Romans 1:1-7

When Paul saw them, he was encouraged and thanked God.
Acts 28:15

_____ , Paul's boat crashed against the rocks. It was a scary time. But God helped Paul and all the other men. Everyone made it safely to shore. The tired men looked all around. "We're on an island!" they said. (An island is land with water on every side. You can't walk to an island. You have to swim or ride in a boat.) They stayed on the island for three long months. Paul had a good time while he was there, but he was glad to go. He wanted to sail for Rome.

After the three long months on the island, Paul climbed on a different boat and set sail. He was excited. Three years before, Paul had sent a letter to the people in Rome who believed in Jesus. We can read that letter, the book of Romans, in the Bible. Paul wanted to see all those people.

When Paul's boat finally reached Rome, he said, "Thanks, God, for making my dream true."

Paul lived in a house in Rome for two years. Many people visited him. No one tried to stop him from talking about Jesus.

Questions
1. What do we call land with water on all sides? (An island)
2. Whom did Paul want to see in Rome? (People who believed in Jesus)

Activity
Look up one or two of these verses in Romans to see what Paul wrote in his letter.
- From Romans 1:8 — I thank my God for you.
- From Romans 8:38, 39 — Nothing can take away God's love.
- From Romans 10:9, 10 — Believe in Jesus.
- From Romans 12:10, 13 — Love and share with each other.
- From Romans 15:13, 32 — I pray for you and want to come see you.

Prayer
Dear God, thanks for sharing Paul's letter to the Romans with us. We can read it, too, and learn more about Jesus. Amen.

A LETTER FROM PAUL
Romans 1:1, 7, 8, 12; 12:9-18

This letter is to all of you in Rome whom God loves. *Romans 1:7*

_____ , do you like to get mail? So do I. Paul wrote lots of letters. Many of his letters are copied down in the Bible. This is part of one letter he wrote:

Dear friends in Rome,
Your love and faith in God make me happy. Keep on loving one another. Work hard and don't be lazy. Be happy because Jesus loves you. When trouble comes, be patient. Pray every day. Share your money and food with those who need help.

When your friend is happy, laugh with him. If your friend is sad, listen to him. If someone is mean to you, don't try to be mean back. Do good things for your friends. God will help you.
Love, Paul

Paul wrote these words many years ago. They are still good for us today. We can read, listen, and learn.

Questions
1. Who wrote a letter to Jesus' followers in Rome? (Paul)
2. What did the letter say? (*Any related answer is fine.* Pray; work hard; do good things; love one another; be happy; Jesus loves you; share; God will help you.)

Activities
1. Plan to take some food to a community organization or food pantry that helps hungry people.
2. Write a letter to a friend or relative.

Prayer
Dear God, I know you love and accept me all the time — even when I forget to be kind and nice. But I'm asking that you help me learn to love others, share, and remember to pray every day. You are a good God, and I know you will help me. Amen.

BEING DIFFERENT IS OK
1 Corinthians 12:4-11

*There are different ways to serve; but all these ways
are from the same Lord. 1 Corinthians 12:4*

Jesus' friends don't all look alike. Some are young. Some are old. Some are tall and others are short. Some have black skin. Some have white skin. Some are girls and others are boys. Many have black hair, but some have red hair. Others have blond or brown hair. A few have no hair at all.

Jesus' friends don't all act the same way, either. God gives us different talents and gifts. Some like to talk. Others like to listen and be quiet. Some like to teach. Others like to help by making things. Some people like to be the leader. Some would rather follow a leader. Some like to play loud games. Others like to read and play quiet games.

_____ , you are different from your friend _____ . God made you that way. We don't all need to look, act, or show our love for Jesus in the same way. God loves us just the way we are. Each person is special to God.

Questions
1. Are Jesus' friends all just alike? (No)
2. Who made us all to look and act different? (God)

Activities
1. Name five friends. What color hair does each friend have?
2. Name two things that you like to do. Name two things that Mom (Dad, brother, or sister) likes to do.

Prayer
Dear God, you made each one of us to be special. I don't have to be just like my friend. I don't have to be just like my dad. I can be me. I'm glad. Thank you. Amen.

LOVE IS A GOOD THING
1 Corinthians 13:4-8

Love never ends. 1 Corinthians 13:8

_____ , have you ever been to a wedding? Jason was going to be in a wedding — his big sister's wedding. He would wear a white suit with a blue bow tie. His special job was to carry the wedding rings. At just the right time, Jason would give the rings to the groom. "Mom, why is Julie marrying Tom?" asked Jason the night before the wedding ceremony.

"Julie loves Tom," said Mom. "And Tom loves Julie."

"What's love?" asked Jason.

"Love is when you care about someone a whole lot," answered Mom.

"Yeah, but I care about you, and I'm not marrying you," said Jason.

Mother smiled. "There are different kinds of love," she said. "Love for friends, parents, children, and love for husbands and wives. But all love is the same in some ways. The Bible says love acts kind and doesn't get mad if the other person is slow doing something. A person who loves doesn't need to have his own way all the time. Love tells the truth. People who love believe one another. And love never stops. Love is a good thing."

"Love is a good thing," repeated Jason. Then he went to sleep.

Questions
1. Who was going to carry the rings in his sister's wedding? (Jason)
2. Does the Bible teach us about love? (Yes)

Activity
Hold a small pillow and walk around the house pretending to carry the wedding rings.

Prayer
Dear God, help me to show love to the people I care about. Amen.

"BUT I WANT TO"
2 Corinthians 9:1-9

Each one should give, then, what he has decided
in his heart to give. *2 Corinthians 9:7*

"I don't have much money left," said Donny. He reached in his pocket and pulled out one dime, one nickel, and five pennies.

"How much do I have?" Donny asked his brother David.

"Well, let's count," said David. "Ten pennies in one dime, five pennies in one nickel. When we add up ten, five, and five, we have twenty. Twenty pennies in all."

"I want to give ten pennies to the kids in Haiti," said Donny. Donny's school was collecting money to send clothes and food to children in the country of Haiti.

"You don't have to do that," said David. "We could buy and share some candy."

"But I want to give it," said Donny.

"Well, OK then," said David. "You can give one dime or one nickel and five pennies. Both equal ten pennies."

_____ , Donny liked giving his ten pennies. It's fun to give to others!

Questions
1. Who had one dime, one nickel, and five pennies in his pocket? (Donny)
2. Did Donny want to give ten pennies to the poor children in Haiti? (Yes)

Activities
1. Count the pennies that you have.
2. Put a small glass jar on a shelf in your child's room. Each day add several pennies. In a few weeks count the money. Then give it to a charity.

Prayer
Dear God, I have so many nice things. Thank you for my food and clothes. I want to share part of what I have with others. Please help me. Thank you. Amen.

YESTERDAY, TODAY, TOMORROW
Hebrews 13:5, 6, 8

Jesus Christ is the same yesterday, today, and forever.
Hebrews 13:8

_____ , what did you do yesterday? *(Pause for a response.)* What have you done today? *(Wait for a response.)* We don't know exactly what we'll do tomorrow, do we? We don't know just how we'll feel, either, do we?

We change. Boys and girls change; moms and dads change; teachers change. Some days we feel happy; other days we may feel sad. Some days we feel more like sharing than other days. Some days we have lots of energy; other days we are tired. One day we may feel sick, but on other days we don't feel sick at all.

We change because we are just people. But Jesus never changes. He is just the same today as he was yesterday, last week, and last year. And he is the same today as he will be when we grow up.

Jesus always loves us. He always wants to help us. He always cares what we are doing and thinking. Jesus is never in a good mood one day and grouchy the next. When Jesus says he will help us, he doesn't change his mind tomorrow.

Jesus treats us in the same loving way every day. I'm glad. Aren't you?

Questions
1. Who is the same yesterday, today, and tomorrow? (Jesus)
2. Do you and I change from day to day? (Yes)
3. Does Jesus always love and care about us? (Yes)
4. Does Jesus ever have a grouchy day? (No)

Activities
1. Write down the days of the week. Which day was yesterday? Which one was today? Which one will be tomorrow?
2. Make a simple calendar of your week's events. Check each day off as you complete it. Mark the calendar as you change plans. Display the calendar in your child's room.

Prayer
Dear Jesus, thanks for loving me the same today as you did on the day I was born. Amen.

NO MORE TEARS
Revelation 21:1-4

He will wipe away every tear from their eyes. Revelation 21:4

Sometimes we cry when we don't get our way. Sometimes we cry when we fall down and skin our arms and legs. But there are other times when we cry because our heart hurts — when someone we love moves away, when our dog dies, when we feel afraid, when a friend or family member is very sick, or when someone we love hurts us. Pain, sickness, divorce, and death can make us feel like crying. Boys and girls cry, moms and dads cry, big sisters and brothers cry, grandmas and grandpas cry.

But one day there will be no more tears for friends of Jesus. That's because he will wipe away all tears. We will live with Jesus in a place where there is no pain, sickness, divorce, or death. We don't know how he will do this. We don't know just when it will happen. Still we believe that it will happen because Jesus said so. _____ , it will be a great day!

Questions
1. What are some things that make us cry?
2. Who will someday wipe away all tears? (Jesus)

Activities
1. Get a tissue and pretend to wipe away your tears.
2. Draw a picture of a crying face. Draw a picture of a happy face.

Prayer
Dear God, sometimes I feel like crying. I know you love me even when I cry. But I'm glad that one day I'll never cry again. Someday I'll be with you and all of your friends forever. That's good. Amen.

96 short, simple devotions for children ages 3-6

Help your child discover the importance and joy of spending time with God.

Devotions for Little Boys and Girls shows you how to structure a devotional time with your children. Each devotion includes a Scripture to discuss, an activity to help children remember what they've learned, and a prayer thanking God for how he worked in the lives of Bible people and how he cares for us today.